Introduction · One world?

The Earth photographed from space in 1972.

Look at the picture above. When Earth is seen from so far away it is obvious that its people share one world. On Earth itself the things that divide people are more obvious than those that unite them. The planet's 5,500 million inhabitants speak about 5,000 languages. They have different religious beliefs and different cultures. They live in different countries, each with different laws and ruled by different types of government.

Above all, they fight one another. Between 1945 and 1985 more than 19 million people were killed in conflicts throughout the world. And this was at a time when nations were, in theory at least, trying to resolve their conflicts peacefully, rather than through war.

This book is about that effort. The United Nations (UN) was founded in 1945 in an attempt to prevent wars and to help nations to co-operate in tackling some of the major problems facing the world after the Second World War. The UN offered the vision that the inhabitants of the Earth live in one world and can work together for their common good.

The world changed very rapidly in the 40 years after 1945, so that the UN of 1985 was a very different organisation from the one that its founders had intended. The question asked by critics as the UN celebrated its fortieth anniversary was, how effective had it been in putting its vision into practice? Did it still play a useful part in world affairs? Some answered, 'no'.

This book will help you to make up your own mind. If so many people died in wars in its first 40 years it is obvious that the UN failed to stop conflict altogether. But might things have been even worse without it? And how successful was the UN in helping to solve other problems such as disease, malnutrition and poverty?

Unit 1 · The United Nations Organisation

1.1 The origins of the United Nations

Wartime devastation. Homeless families wander through the streets of Berlin in search of shelter.

Hopes for a better future

More than 50 million people were killed in the Second World War. Hundreds of cities were devastated (Source 1). Millions of people became refugees. By 1945 there was a desperate desire for a lasting peace and a hope that nations might co-operate to create a better world.

These had also been people's hopes 26 years before, when the First World War had ended. The peace treaties of 1919 had set up the League of Nations, which was intended to check acts of aggression and prevent war. It had been only partly successful. In 1945 people wanted a much stronger organisation with wider membership (the USA, for example, had not joined the League) and with the ability to use military force if necessary.

The Atlantic Charter, 1941

The idea for a new organisation to help international co-operation in the future was born during the Second World War itself. In June 1941 a number of nations fighting Hitler agreed to set one up after the war. That August Winston Churchill, the British Prime Minister, and Franklin Roosevelt, President of the United States, met on a warship in the Atlantic Ocean to discuss the future of the world at the end of the war.

The two leaders produced a declaration called the Atlantic Charter. This outlined eight 'hopes for the better future of the world', especially the hopes that all countries would have democratic governments and that they would trade freely with each other and share economic prosperity. It spoke of a 'wider and permanent system of general security' which would:

Source 2

The Atlantic Charter, 14 August 1941.

> Afford to all nations the means of dwelling in safety within their own boundaries.

The United Nations Declaration, 1942

The USA was not at war when the Atlantic Charter was signed, but within four months it was fighting Japan, one of Germany's allies. Roosevelt suggested that all the states at war with the Axis Powers (Germany and its allies) should call themselves the United Nations (Source 4). In January 1942, 26 of them signed a United Nations Declaration which said that they supported the ideals of the Atlantic Charter and would continue to co-operate after the war.

Wartime conferences, 1943–1945

Four of the United Nations were more powerful than the rest. The USA, Britain, the USSR and China were known as the 'Big Four'. In October 1943 they met in Moscow and agreed to set up a 'General International Organisation' as soon as possible.

The following year officials and diplomats of the Big Four met at Dumbarton Oaks, a large house near Washington. There they planned the details of the organisation. They proposed that:

Source 3

From the proposed aims of the UN, published after the Dumbarton Oaks Conference, 1944.

There should be established an international organisation under the title of the United Nations . . . .

The purposes of this organisation should be:

1 To maintain international peace and security . . .
2 To develop friendly relations among nations . . .
3 . . . the solution of international economic, social and other humanitarian problems.
4 To afford a centre for harmonizing the actions of nations in the achievement of these common ends.

Source 4

A Second World War poster celebrating the struggle of the 'United Nations' against the Axis Powers.

THE UNITED NATIONS FIGHT FOR FREEDOM

■ What do Sources 1, 3 and the information in the text about the new specialised agencies tell you about the problems facing the world as a result of the Second World War?

In 1945, Churchill, Roosevelt and Stalin, the Soviet leader, met in Yalta in the Crimea where they discussed voting arrangements for the United Nations Organisation and how decisions would be made. They agreed that all states which had declared war on the Axis Powers by 1 March 1945 should qualify for founder membership of the UN. Each state would have one vote in a General Assembly. Self-governing dominions of the British Empire, such as Canada and Australia were to have separate votes from Britain, even though they were not independent. Also two Soviet republics, the Ukraine and Byelorussia, were to have separate votes from the Soviet Union.

They also decided that each of the Big Four would have the right to veto certain decisions (later they added France, to make it the Big Five). This meant that a decision could only be made if they all agreed to it. If one of them disagreed it could not be put into effect.

New specialised agencies

Wartime conferences also set up various agencies to deal with particular problems caused by the war. In 1943, for example, a Food and Agricultural Organisation (FAO) was set up to organise food supplies, and the United Nations Relief and Rehabilitation Administration (UNRRA) was established to bring food and medical care to European people living in areas devastated by the war.

An International Bank and an International Monetary Fund (IMF) were also founded in 1944 to help trade and economic development after the war. The idea grew up that the United Nations should co-ordinate the work of this 'family' of specialist organisations.

The San Francisco Conference, 1945

In 1945 the war in Europe was nearly over; and in the Pacific the Japanese were in retreat. That April, delegates from 49 of the United Nations met in San Francisco to discuss the Charter, or set of rules, of the United Nations Organisation. At the opening ceremony they heard Harry S. Truman, the new President of the United States tell them:

Source 5

The Times, 26 April 1945.

The essence of our problem here is to provide sensible machinery for the settlement of disputes among nations. Without this peace cannot exist. We can no longer permit any nation, or group of nations, to attempt to settle their arguments with bombs or bayonets.

Source 6

Delegates from China signing the Charter of the United Nations in San Francisco's Opera House on 25 June 1945.

Each delegation signed the Charter in turn. The original 49 delegations were joined in the course of the Conference by Argentina and by Poland, so 51 countries became founder members. Two months later, on 25 June 1945, they took part in a ceremony to sign the Charter (Source 6). Its opening words stated:

Source 7

From the Charter of the United Nations, 1945.

We, the people of the United Nations, [are] determined to save succeeding generations from the scourge of war, which twice in our lifetime has brought untold sorrow to mankind, and . . . to employ international machinery for the promotion of the economic and social advancement of all people.

Questions

1   Make a timeline of the events which led to the creation of the United Nations Organisation and write brief notes to say what happened at each event.

2   a) Here are two reasons why the United Nations Organisation was set up: (i) the impact of the Second World War; (ii) the attitudes of the Big Four. Write a paragraph about each one.
b) What other reasons were there? Make a list of your ideas and write a paragraph about each one.
c) Using your notes from parts a) and b), write an essay to explain why and how the United Nations Organisation came to be set up in 1945.

3   a) What do you think were the main motives of the leaders of Britain, the USA and the USSR in founding the UN?
b) Which motives do you think were the strongest? Give your reasons.

1.2 The UN system

The UN's Charter described the work the UN was to do and explained how the organisation would function. It set up a General Assembly, a Security Council, an Economic and Social Council, a Trusteeship Council, an International Court of Justice and a Secretariat (Source 8). All these are based in New York except the International Court of Justice, which meets in The Hague, in the Netherlands.

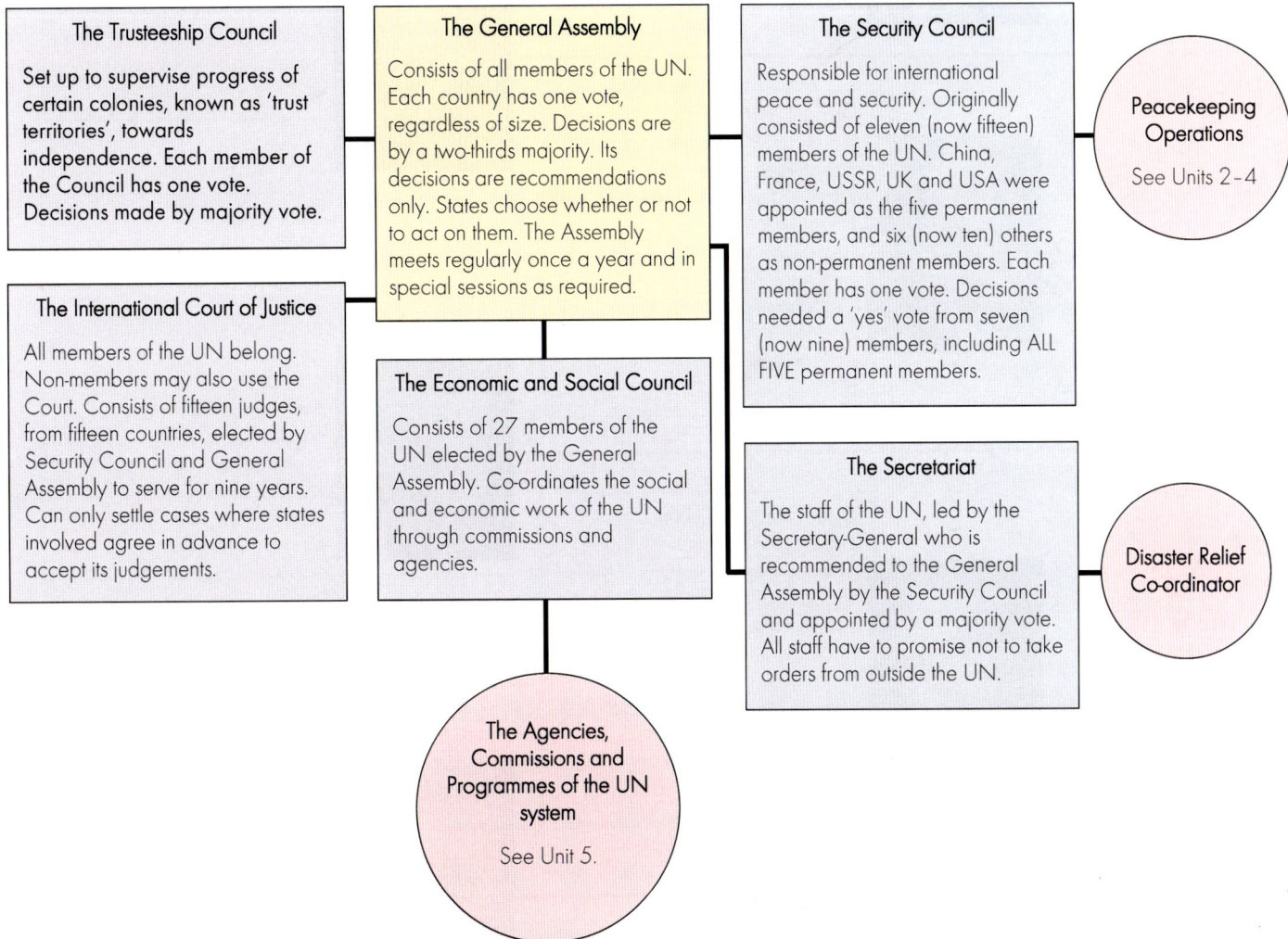

The Trusteeship Council

Set up to supervise progress of certain colonies, known as 'trust territories', towards independence. Each member of the Council has one vote. Decisions made by majority vote.

The International Court of Justice

All members of the UN belong. Non-members may also use the Court. Consists of fifteen judges, from fifteen countries, elected by Security Council and General Assembly to serve for nine years. Can only settle cases where states involved agree in advance to accept its judgements.

The General Assembly

Consists of all members of the UN. Each country has one vote, regardless of size. Decisions are by a two-thirds majority. Its decisions are recommendations only. States choose whether or not to act on them. The Assembly meets regularly once a year and in special sessions as required.

The Economic and Social Council

Consists of 27 members of the UN elected by the General Assembly. Co-ordinates the social and economic work of the UN through commissions and agencies.

The Security Council

Responsible for international peace and security. Originally consisted of eleven (now fifteen) members of the UN. China, France, USSR, UK and USA were appointed as the five permanent members, and six (now ten) others as non-permanent members. Each member has one vote. Decisions needed a 'yes' vote from seven (now nine) members, including ALL FIVE permanent members.

Peacekeeping Operations

See Units 2–4

The Secretariat

The staff of the UN, led by the Secretary-General who is recommended to the General Assembly by the Security Council and appointed by a majority vote. All staff have to promise not to take orders from outside the UN.

Disaster Relief Co-ordinator

The Agencies, Commissions and Programmes of the UN system

See Unit 5.

The Secretary-General

The Secretary-General is the head of the UN's Secretariat. He or she is elected for five years and can be re-elected for a further five. The job of the Secretary-General is to:
- manage the whole UN organisation;
- draw the attention of the Security Council to any problem affecting the peace of the world;
- use his or her good offices to help to resolve international disputes;
- lead UN missions to any area to take over UN activities there.

So far there have been six Secretaries-General (Source 9).

Source 9

The Secretaries-General of the UN, 1946–present.

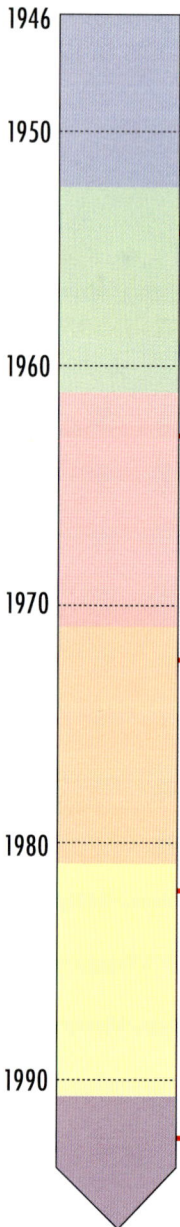

1946

1950

1960

1970

1980

1990

Trygve Lie, 1946–1953. From Norway. Previously Foreign Minister of Norway. He had to cope with the beginning of the 'Cold War', the UN's first international crises, and the Korean War. In 1950 the Soviet Union accused him of bias in favour of the West (the USA and its allies) and against the East (the USSR and its communist allies). He resigned in 1953.

Dag Hammarskjöld, 1953–1961. From Sweden. Previously an economist and diplomat. He aimed to be strictly neutral. He increased the influence of the office of UN Secretary-General and dealt with major crises in the Middle East and the Congo where he died in an air crash in 1961. Like Lie, he was accused by the USSR of bias against communist countries and in favour of the West.

U Thant, 1962–1971. From Burma (now Myanmar). Previously a diplomat. He continued to build up the authority of the office and to be neutral and unbiased. He was involved in the Cuban Missiles Crisis, helped to solve the Congo Crisis and dealt with crises in Cyprus and the Middle East.

Kurt Waldheim, 1972–1981. From Austria. Previously a politician and diplomat. His period of office saw crises in the Middle East, Cyprus and Afghanistan. He was elected President of Austria in 1986 but his presidency was overshadowed by allegations that during the Second World War he had been in a German Army unit responsible for transporting Jews to death camps.

Javier Pérez de Cuéllar, 1982–1991. From Peru. Previously a diplomat. His period of office saw the Falklands War, a crisis in the Lebanon, the break-up of the communist group of countries in East Europe in 1989 and the start of the break-up of the USSR in 1991. It was dominated by the eight-year Gulf War between Iran and Iraq which ended when he negotiated a cease-fire in 1988.

Boutros Boutros-Ghali, 1992–present. From Egypt. Previously a diplomat and politician. Under his leadership the UN has attempted to deal with major crises in the former Yugoslavia and in Somalia.

Questions

1 Look at the aims of the UN in Source 3 (page 3). Then study Source 8 on page 5. Taking each part of the organisation in turn, what role do you think it has in helping to achieve the UN's aims?

2 Describe the aims of the founders of the UN and explain how the organisation was set up so that it could carry them out.

3 Using Source 9 and the information about the job of UN Secretary-General, make lists of: a) the skills; b) the personal qualities that you think a Secretary-General needs to have.

Unit 2 · Peacekeeping in a changing world

The founders of the UN assumed that the permanent members of the Security Council – the so-called 'Big Five' of the USA, the USSR, Britain, China and France – would act together as the chief peacekeepers of the world. This did not happen. Within a few months of the opening of the San Francisco Conference, and before the UN's first General Assembly in January 1946, the world situation changed.

Instead of being controlled by five great powers, the world became dominated by two superpowers, the USA and the USSR. And instead of working together, the superpowers faced one another as enemies. For nearly 50 years the world was to live in fear of a war more terrible even than the Second World War.

Thus the very situation that made world peacekeeping all the more vital also meant that the UN could not function in the way its founders had intended. This Unit is about how the rivalry of the superpowers affected the UN, and about how the UN managed to develop its peacekeeping role in the post-war world.

2.1 Early problems

Source 1

The Cold War. This map shows the USSR and its allies (the East) and the USA and its allies (the West) between 1945 and 1959.

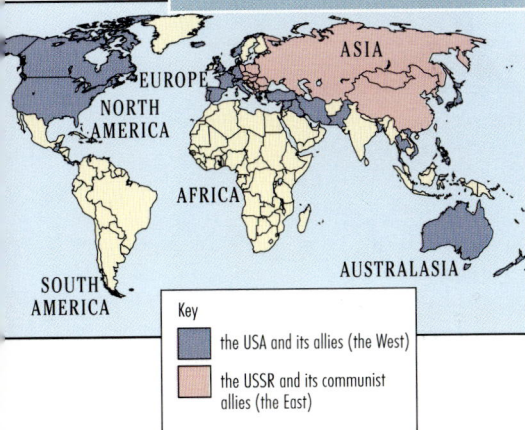

Key
- the USA and its allies (the West)
- the USSR and its communist allies (the East)

■ How did superpower rivalry: a) pose a threat to world peace; b) affect the way the UN was meant to work?

The UN Charter gave the Security Council two ways of dealing with a threat to world peace. The first involved the use of peaceful methods, for example by applying economic sanctions against offenders. This meant that other countries had to stop trading with them so that the offenders would run out of essential goods. The second method involved the use of armed forces.

The Charter set up a Military Staff Committee representing each of the Big Five so that they had joint control of any UN force. In addition, each of the Big Five had the power of veto in the Security Council. That meant they could prevent a UN force being used against themselves or their special allies. Less powerful countries were to play a very small part in keeping world peace.

The 'Cold War'

As it turned out, the 'Cold War' between the USA, the USSR and their allies caused the Big Five to quarrel amongst themselves and gave the less significant nations more influence than anyone had expected.

The start of the Cold War affected the UN in two ways. Firstly, it caused the members of the Military Staff Committee to fail to agree about how to set up a UN force for the use of the Security Council. Secondly, it meant that the Big Five were unable to act together as the world's police force. Instead, the USA and the USSR were likely to use world crises to score points off one another, and they could use their vetoes to block any peacekeeping decisions they did not like. Security Council meetings became extensions of the Cold War itself.

Source 2

The UN and world crises, 1945–1949

2a Berlin

In 1945 Germany was divided into four zones. Britain, France, the USA and the USSR controlled one each. The capital, Berlin, was similarly divided. The USSR refused to co-operate with plans for a democratic government for the whole of Germany. In June 1948 the three Western Allies began reforms on their own. The USSR banned trade between its zone and the rest, and blockaded West Berlin, aiming to take it over. The Western Allies flew in supplies in a massive 'Berlin airlift' and appealed to the UN. War threatened. The non-permanent members of Security Council attempted mediation, which failed. The Secretary-General then brought the four powers together in private talks. These, together with failure of Soviet blockade, led to an agreement over Berlin.

Key

- Communist rebel-held areas
- The Balkan region
- Main supply routes to rebel areas
- UN UNSCOB positions

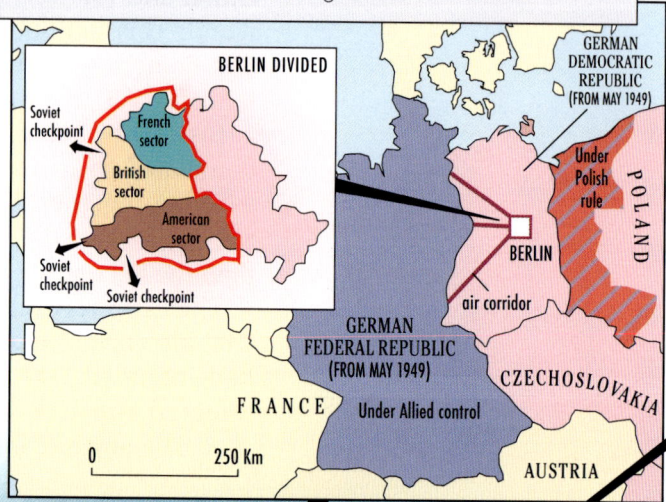

YUGOSLAVIA

River Danube

BULGARIA

ALBANIA

GREECE

Training camp for Greek rebels

British troops in Athens help train the Greek Army to fight rebels. British government supplies arms and equipment.

BERLIN DIVIDED

Soviet checkpoint

French sector

British sector

American sector

Soviet checkpoint

Soviet checkpoint

GERMAN DEMOCRATIC REPUBLIC (FROM MAY 1949)

Under Polish rule

P O L A N D

BERLIN

air corridor

GERMAN FEDERAL REPUBLIC (FROM MAY 1949)

F R A N C E

Under Allied control

CZECHOSLOVAKIA

AUSTRIA

0   250 Km

2b Greece

British troops were sent to free Greece from German troops in 1944. They remained after the war, at the request of the Greek government, to fight communist rebels. In 1947 the Security Council dismissed a Soviet complaint that Britain was interfering in the affairs of Greece. Greece then complained that communist Yugoslavia, Albania and Bulgaria were supporting the rebels. The UN ordered them to stop and set up a Special Committee on the Balkans (UNSCOB) to monitor the situation. The USSR, Yugoslavia, Bulgaria and Albania refused to deal with UNSCOB, which reported continued communist support for the rebels. UN efforts to hold peace talks failed. The fighting ended only after Yugoslavia stopped supporting the rebels in 1948.

The first crises, 1945–1949

The first issues of peace and security which the UN had to deal with arose directly out of circumstances following the end of the Second World War (Source 2). Several involved members of the Security Council and either arose out directly out of the Cold War (2a) or else quickly got involved in it. For instance, the USSR assumed Iran's complaint against it (2d) was set in motion by the USA and, therefore, retaliated with a complaint against the USA's chief ally, Britain (2b). The crises in Indonesia (2e) and Palestine (2c) stemmed from the desire of subject peoples (or, in the case of the Jews, a people without a state) to set up their own independent nations.

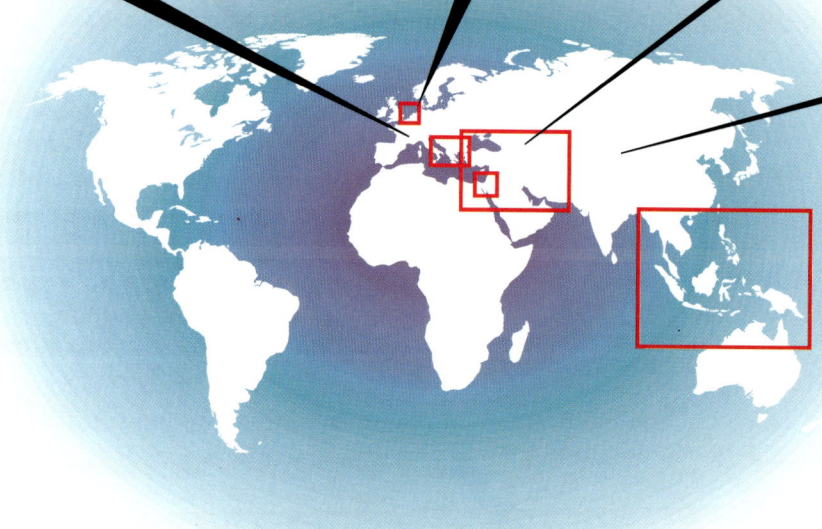

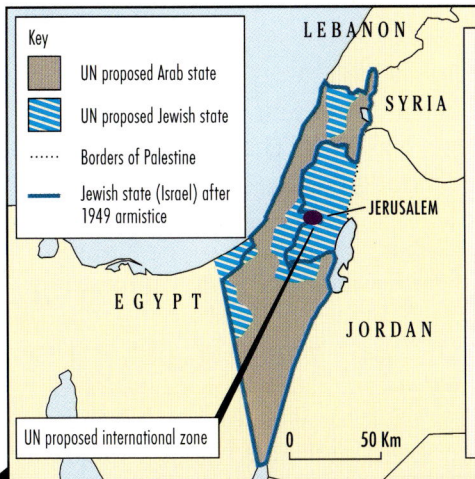

Key

- ▨ UN proposed Arab state
- ▨ UN proposed Jewish state
- ···· Borders of Palestine
- ── Jewish state (Israel) after 1949 armistice

LEBANON

SYRIA

JERUSALEM

EGYPT

JORDAN

UN proposed international zone

0   50 Km

2c Palestine

From 1922 Britain governed the Arab state of Palestine but supported the Jews' demand for it to become their 'national home'. As Jewish immigration increased so did fighting between Arabs and Jews. In 1947 the British, hated by both sides, asked the UN to take responsibility. A General Assembly Special Committee devised a plan to divide Palestine into a Jewish and an Arab state. Despite Arab opposition, the UN accepted the plan. Fighting increased. When the British withdrew in May 1948 the Jews set up a separate state of Israel in areas given to them in the UN plan. Surrounding Arab states invaded. The UN arranged a truce. After more fighting, the Israelis were victorious. In 1949 the UN organised a new truce. Israel and four of its five Arab opponents signed, but the Arabs still refused to recognise Israel.

TURKEY

SYRIA

IRAQ

SAUDI ARABIA

Republic of Azerbaijan

USSR

Kurdish Republic

IRAN

AFGHANISTAN

0   500 Km

2d Iran

Soviet and British troops were stationed in Iran during the war to secure oil for Allied use. Angry that the Iranians refused to grant them special rights to oil after the war, the Soviets failed to leave. They remained in the North, where they helped rebels set up two breakaway states, the Republic of Azerbaijan and the Kurdish Republic. In January 1946 Iran complained to the UN about Soviet interference in its internal affairs. The Security Council discussed the issue and asked to be kept informed about the progress of talks between Soviets and Iranians. This kept up pressure on the USSR. The Iranian government negotiated the withdrawal of Soviet troops (May 1946) and later regained control of the northern provinces.

2e Indonesia

Indonesia was a Dutch colony, occupied during the war by the Japanese. After the war Nationalists set up an independent republic, but the Dutch sent troops to reclaim the colony. In 1947 the UN intervened. The Dutch said the UN had no right to interfere in a 'domestic matter'. Nevertheless, the Security Council ordered a cease-fire. Both sides obeyed. The UN then set up a committee to settle the dispute. Both sides agreed to share the government of Indonesia, but negotiations broke down. In 1948 the Dutch attacked the Republicans again. The Security Council called for full independence for Indonesia. The Dutch objected, found themselves without support and agreed to a UN proposal for a peace conference. As a result, the Dutch granted independence to Indonesia in 1949.

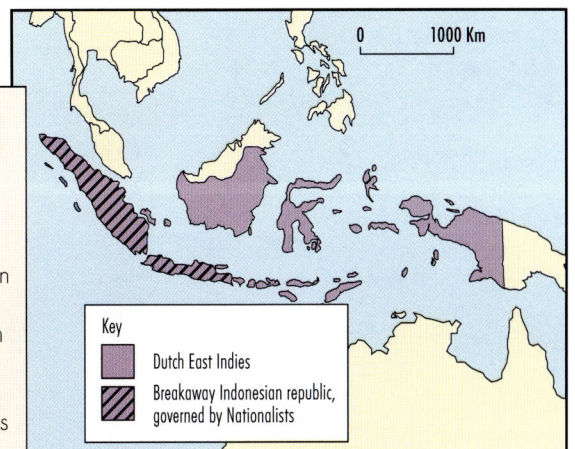

0   1000 Km

Key

- ▨ Dutch East Indies
- ▨ Breakaway Indonesian republic, governed by Nationalists

Questions

1 Ask your teacher for a copy of the chart 'Forms of UN action'. Complete the chart, following the instructions at the top of the sheet.

2 a) Use your completed chart for Question 1 to help you to make a list of the arguments that support the view that the UN's first four years as a peacekeeping organisation were: (i) successful; (ii) unsuccessful.
b) Which view do you agree with? Explain your answer.

2.2 The Korean War

On Saturday 24 June 1954, Harry Truman, President of the USA, was at home with his family in Independence, Missouri. That night he received news that plunged the world and the UN into crisis:

Source 3

From H. S. Truman's autobiography, *Years of Trial and Hope 1946–1953*, published in 1956.

It was a little after ten in the evening and we were sitting in the library . . . when the telephone rang. It was the Secretary of State calling from his home in Maryland.

'Mr President,' said Dean Acheson, 'I have very serious news. The North Koreans have invaded South Korea.'

My first reaction was that I must get back to [Washington] . . . I had time to think aboard the plane. In my generation this was not the first occasion when the strong had attacked the weak . . . I remembered how each time that the democracies failed to act, it had encouraged the aggressors to keep going ahead. Communism was acting in Korea just as Hitler, Mussolini and the Japanese had acted ten, fifteen and twenty years earlier . . . the foundations and principles of the United Nations were at stake.

Background to the invasion

Korea became a Japanese colony in 1910. When Japan surrendered to the Allies in 1945 Soviet troops occupied northern Korea and American troops the South. Their two governments agreed that the line of latitude 38° North (known as the 38th Parallel) should be the dividing line between the two areas of occupation; but within two years it had become the line dividing separate countries (Source 4).

Source 4

Events in the Far East, 1945–1949.

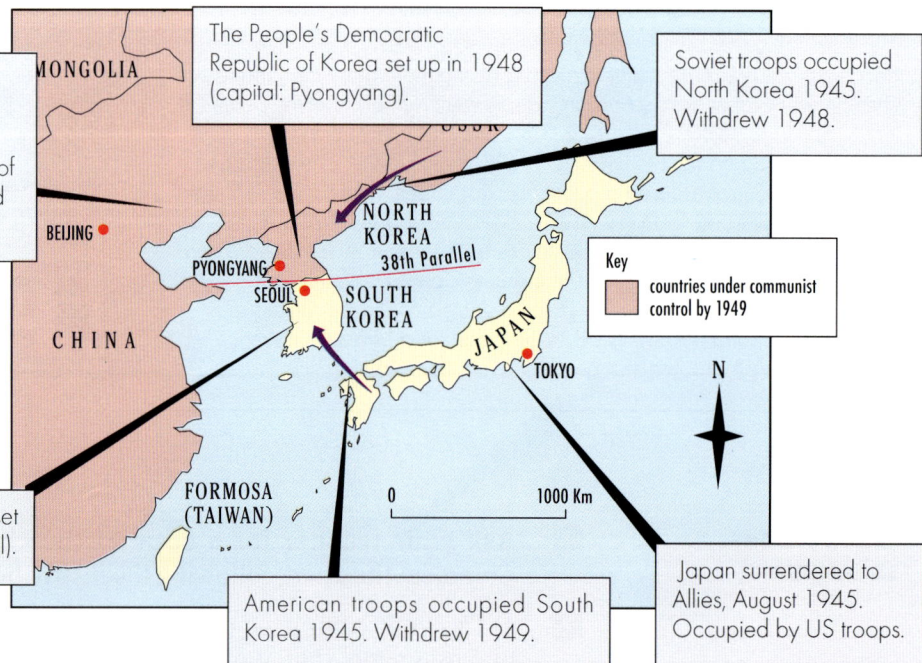

The People's Democratic Republic of Korea set up in 1948 (capital: Pyongyang).

Soviet troops occupied North Korea 1945. Withdrew 1948.

From 1945 Nationalists fought Communists in civil war which ended with communist victory in 1949. Communists set up People's Republic of China. Nationalists fled to Taiwan and set up Republic of China.

Key
countries under communist control by 1949

The Republic of Korea set up in 1948 (capital: Seoul).

American troops occupied South Korea 1945. Withdrew 1949.

Japan surrendered to Allies, August 1945. Occupied by US troops.

In 1947 the UN General Assembly decided that elections should be held throughout Korea to choose a national government. It set up a UN Commission to supervise the elections, but the Soviet authorities in the

North refused to co-operate. Voters in the South elected a parliament which set up the government of the Republic of Korea. The UN Commission said that these elections had been fair.

In the North the Communists set up the government of the People's Democratic Republic of Korea. Since the UN had not been allowed to observe elections there, the General Assembly declared that the government in the South was the only freely elected and lawful government in Korea. Whatever the UN said, there were now two Koreas; and the 38th Parallel was the frontier between them.

The two republics each claimed to rule the whole of Korea. Their armies clashed several times near the 38th Parallel during 1948–1950. The USA and USSR withdrew their troops, but continued to give money and weapons to the two sides; the USA to the South and the USSR to the North.

UN Observers kept watch along the 38th Parallel. At dawn on 25 June (the evening of 24 June in the USA, because of a difference in dates created by the International Date Line) they saw North Korean troops launch a massive surprise attack across the border.

The UN's response

At 3 a.m. on 25 July the USA's ambassador to the UN phoned the Secretary-General, Trygve Lie, to ask him to call the Security Council together as soon as possible. Lie had already heard the news of the North Korean attack and had called for full reports from the UN observers. What he heard convinced him that this was:

Source 5

From Trygve Lie's account of his time as UN Secretary-General, *In the Cause of Peace,* 1954.

> . . . clear-cut aggression – apparently well calculated, meticulously planned, and with all the elements of surprise which reminded me of the Nazi invasion of Norway . . . aggression against a 'creation' of the United Nations . . .

When the Security Council met that afternoon, the Soviet delegation was not present. It had been absent since January, in protest against China being represented at the UN by the nationalist government in Taiwan, rather than by the communist government in Beijing (see Source 4).

The USA put forward a resolution stating that the North Koreans had breached world peace and calling on them to withdraw to the 38th Parallel. Nine members supported this resolution and one abstained. The USSR would have used its right as a permanent member of the Security Council to veto it; but in the absence of its representative it could not do so.

The North Koreans ignored the Council's resolution. Two days later it passed another one, calling on the UN to give South Korea:

Source 6

Security Council resolution, 27 June 1950.

> Such assistance . . . as may be necessary to repel the armed attack and to restore international peace and security in the area.

Again, the Council was able to pass the resolution because the Soviet member was not there to veto it.

The Secretary-General immediately began to contact members of the UN to ask for military help. The forces of sixteen states were brought together in a UN Joint Command. An American general, Douglas MacArthur, was appointed as Commander-in- Chief.

The course of the war

The Korean War fell into four stages. The North Korean army swept the South Koreans back to Pusan (1). UN and South Korean troops then drove the North Koreans back, and, despite warnings from China not to cross the 38th Parallel, advanced almost to the Chinese border (2). The Chinese then entered the war, drove the UN forces back and advanced into South Korea (3). Finally, a counter-attack by UN forces drove the Chinese back again. The two front lines then remained roughly along the 38th Parallel until an armistice was signed at Panmunjom two years later in 1953 (4).

Source 7

The course of the Korean War, 1950–1953.

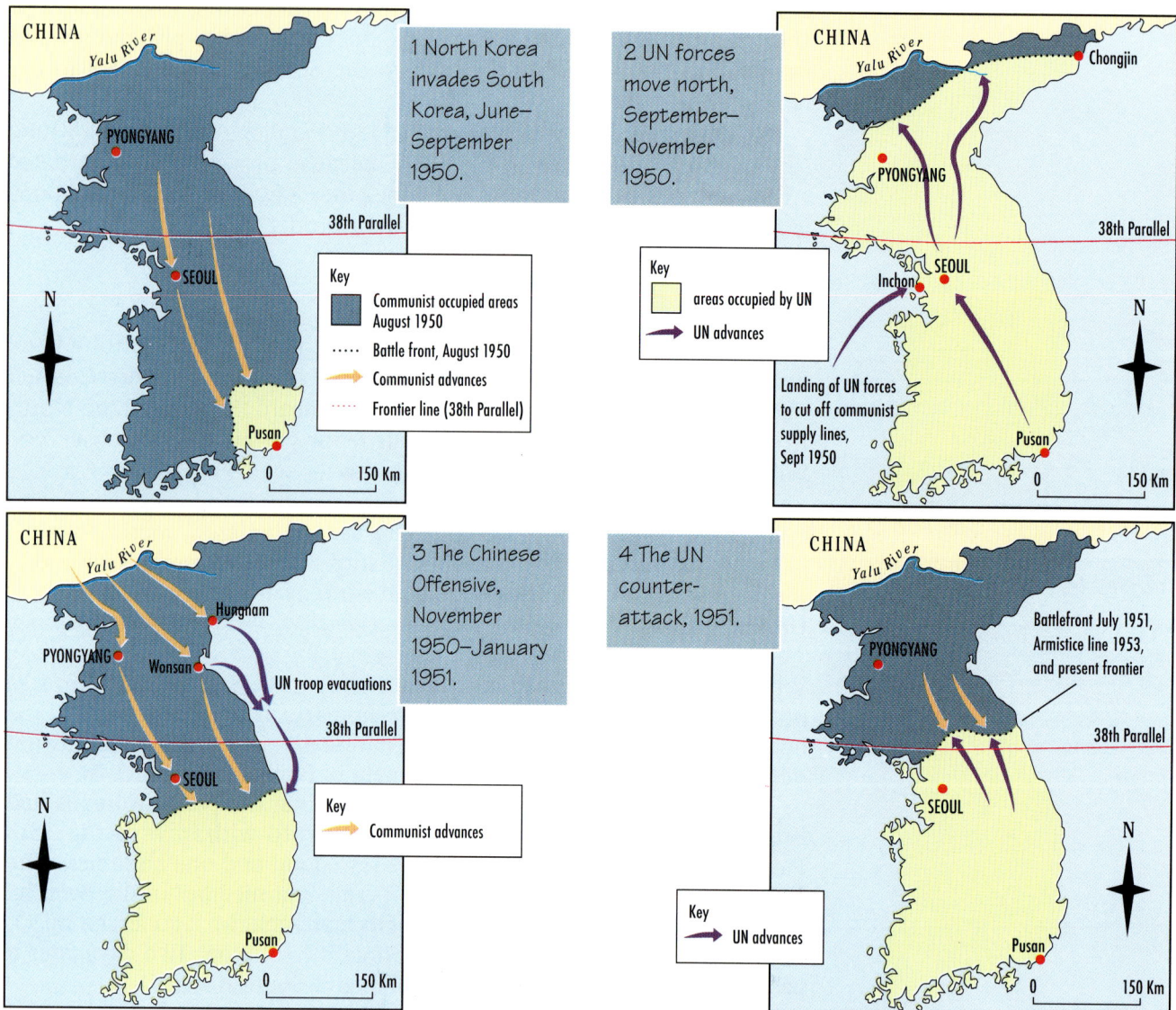

1 North Korea invades South Korea, June–September 1950.

Key
- Communist occupied areas August 1950
- .... Battle front, August 1950
- Communist advances
- ----- Frontier line (38th Parallel)

2 UN forces move north, September–November 1950.

Key
- areas occupied by UN
- UN advances

Landing of UN forces to cut off communist supply lines, Sept 1950

3 The Chinese Offensive, November 1950–January 1951.

UN troop evacuations

Key
- Communist advances

4 The UN counter-attack, 1951.

Battlefront July 1951, Armistice line 1953, and present frontier

Key
- UN advances

Whose war: the USA's or the UN's?

Although sixteen countries contributed forces to the UN operation in Korea, the USA contributed the lion's share. The United States was also given unlimited authority to direct military operations, though it had to give regular reports to the Security Council. It was President Truman who appointed General MacArthur as commander of UN forces. MacArthur reported to the US President and took orders from him and MacArthur's reports to the Security Council always went to the US government first.

As one historian has commented:

Source 8

Evan Luard, *A History of the United Nations, Volume 1*, 1982.

The operation in the eyes of many was not a UN operation in any normal sense but became instead a US operation which happened to enjoy UN endorsement [approval] and support.

Ten other governments offered non-military assistance. Medical care was chiefly supplied by Denmark, India, Israel, Italy, Norway and Sweden. In 1951 the UN forces were made up as follows:

	USA %	South Korea %	Other %
Land forces	50	40	10
Air forces	93	6	1
Naval forces	86	7	7

The legacy of the war

Source 9

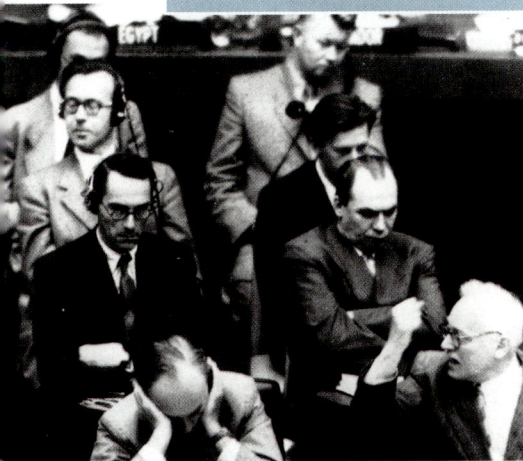

Security Council meeting, 1953. The Korean War increased the split between the communist and non-communist worlds.

Korea
The UN's policy had always been that Korea should become one country with free elections supervised by the UN. The war did nothing to bring this nearer. What it did do was to halt an aggressor and restore the position to what it had been before the North Korean attack.

'Uniting for Peace'
In August 1950 the Soviet delegation once again took its place in the Security Council and started to use its veto to block decisions. The United States then put forward a resolution called 'Uniting for Peace' to the General Assembly. It said that the Assembly could take over responsibility for peacekeeping if the Security Council was unable to act because a decision had been vetoed. The Americans did this because they knew that most UN members supported them on most issues, and no country had a veto in the Assembly. The resolution was passed, but the USSR claimed it was illegal and refused to accept decisions made in this way.

The Secretary-General
The USSR never forgave Trygve Lie for the swift lead he gave in organising the UN's response to the invasion of South Korea. It accused him of supporting the Americans and of acting beyond the limits of his office. The Soviet delegation, therefore, refused to have any further dealings with him. His position became so difficult that, in 1953, he decided to resign.

Questions

1 a) What evidence is there on pages 10–11 that the USA took the lead in the UN's response to the invasion of South Korea?
b) Why do you think that the USA was able to do this?

2 Read Source 8.
a) What evidence is there on pages 10–13 to support this view of the operation in Korea?
b) Is there any evidence to challenge or modify it?

2.3 The impact of new nations

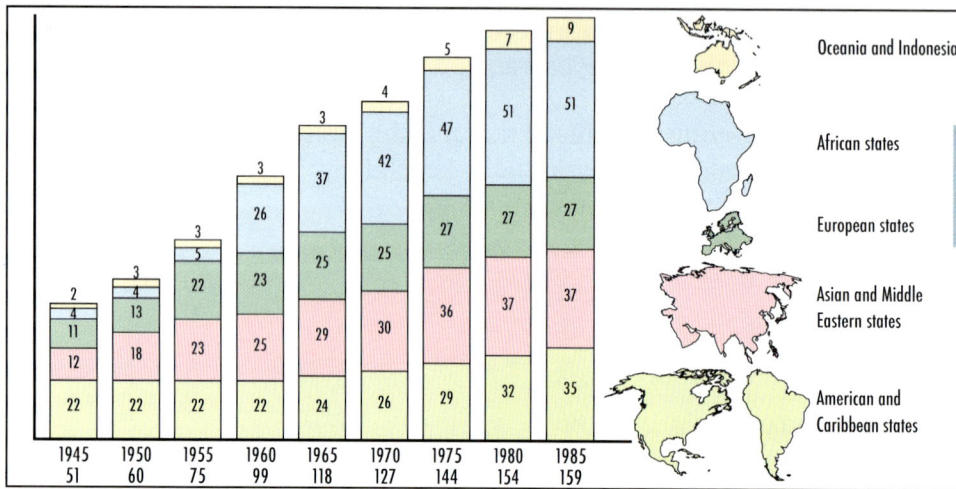

Oceania and Indonesia

African states

European states

Asian and Middle Eastern states

American and Caribbean states

Source 10

The growth of the UN and changes in its membership, 1945–1985.

	1945	1950	1955	1960	1965	1970	1975	1980	1985
Oceania/Indonesia	2	3	3	3	3	4	5	7	9
African	4	4	5	26	37	42	47	51	51
European	11	13	22	23	25	25	27	27	27
Asian/Middle East	12	18	23	25	29	30	36	37	37
American/Caribbean	22	22	22	22	24	26	29	32	35
Total	51	60	75	99	118	127	144	154	159

The expanding UN

In 1945 large parts of the world, especially in Asia and Africa, still belonged to the empires of European states such as Britain and France. After 1945 the Europeans started to give their colonies independence. As each colony became independent it was free to join the UN as a sovereign state, equal to every other member. The membership of the UN increased from 51 in 1945 to 99 in 1960, mainly as a result of newly independent Asian and African states joining it. By 1985 the membership had reached 159 (Source 10).

A Third World

The new nations found themselves confronted by two worlds, the West and the East, one dominated by the USA and the other by the USSR. They found that they were expected to join one world or the other; but many feared the superpowers and mistrusted the idea that either the capitalism of the West or the communism of the East held all the answers. Because as undeveloped countries they were poorer than those in both the West and the East, and because politically they did not wish to join either of the two existing worlds, they came to be known as the Third World.

Non-alignment

Led by the Prime Minister of India, Jawaharlal Nehru, many Third World countries developed a policy of non-alignment. This meant that they aimed to take up a neutral position between the two superpowers and were equally prepared to deal with either. They were also prepared to take up an independent position in the UN.

In 1955 representatives of 29 Asian and African countries met at a conference held in Bandung in Indonesia (Source 11). This conference inspired the setting up, in 1961, of the Non-Aligned Movement, which became an important Third World organisation.

International alignments at the time of the Bandung Conference, 1955.

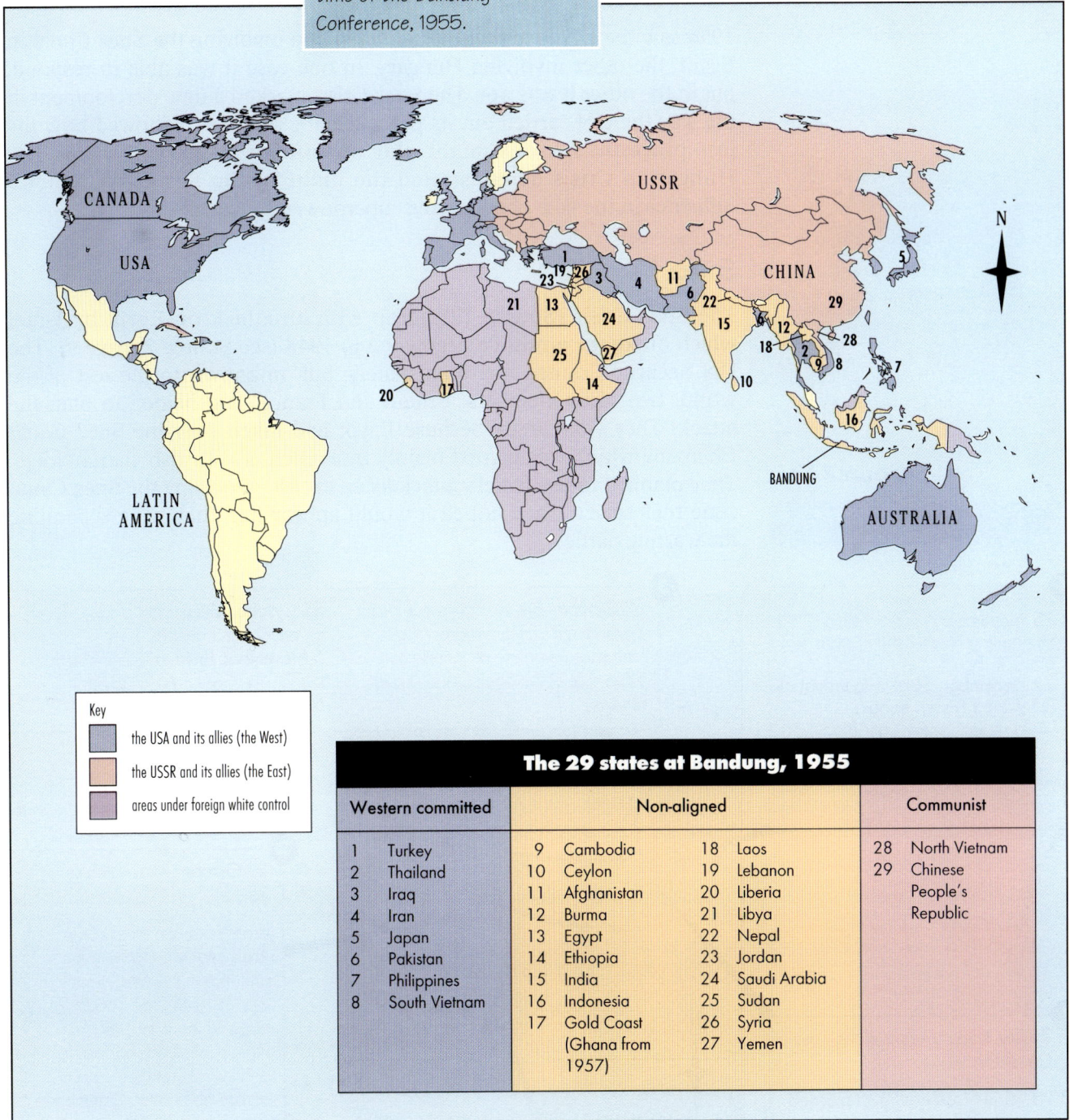

Key
- the USA and its allies (the West)
- the USSR and its allies (the East)
- areas under foreign white control

The 29 states at Bandung, 1955				
Western committed	**Non-aligned**		**Communist**	
1 Turkey	9 Cambodia	18 Laos	28 North Vietnam	
2 Thailand	10 Ceylon	19 Lebanon	29 Chinese	
3 Iraq	11 Afghanistan	20 Liberia	People's	
4 Iran	12 Burma	21 Libya	Republic	
5 Japan	13 Egypt	22 Nepal		
6 Pakistan	14 Ethiopia	23 Jordan		
7 Philippines	15 India	24 Saudi Arabia		
8 South Vietnam	16 Indonesia	25 Sudan		
	17 Gold Coast	26 Syria		
	(Ghana from	27 Yemen		
	1957)			

Non-aligned states made a strong impact on the workings of the UN. Since the foundation of the UN, the Western group of countries, led by the USA, had always been in a majority in the General Assembly. As new Asian and African states joined, so the balance of power within the UN shifted. Without an automatic majority, the USA had to start to take account of the opinions of new members. Equally the USSR saw a chance to increase its following and began to do the same.

2.4 1956: A testing year

1956 saw the UN faced with two crises, one involving the Suez Canal in Egypt, the other involving Hungary. In one case it was able to respond, but in the other it was not. The Suez Crisis marked a new development in the way the UN carried out its peacekeeping duties and showed how the less powerful nations might play an influential part in them. The Hungarian Crisis demonstrated the limits of the Security Council's influence in the face of one of the superpowers.

Suez

The Suez Crisis (Source 12) began with an attack on Egypt by Israel which broke the armistice negotiated in 1948 (see Source 2, page 9). The UN Security Council met immediately; but, unknown to the rest of the world, two of its members, Britain and France, had helped to plan the attack. They were angry because Egypt had taken over the Suez Canal Company which was owned mainly by French and British shareholders. They planned to use Israel's attack as an excuse to occupy the Suez Canal zone themselves. They hoped it would appear that they were separating the warring parties.

Source 12

The Suez Crisis.

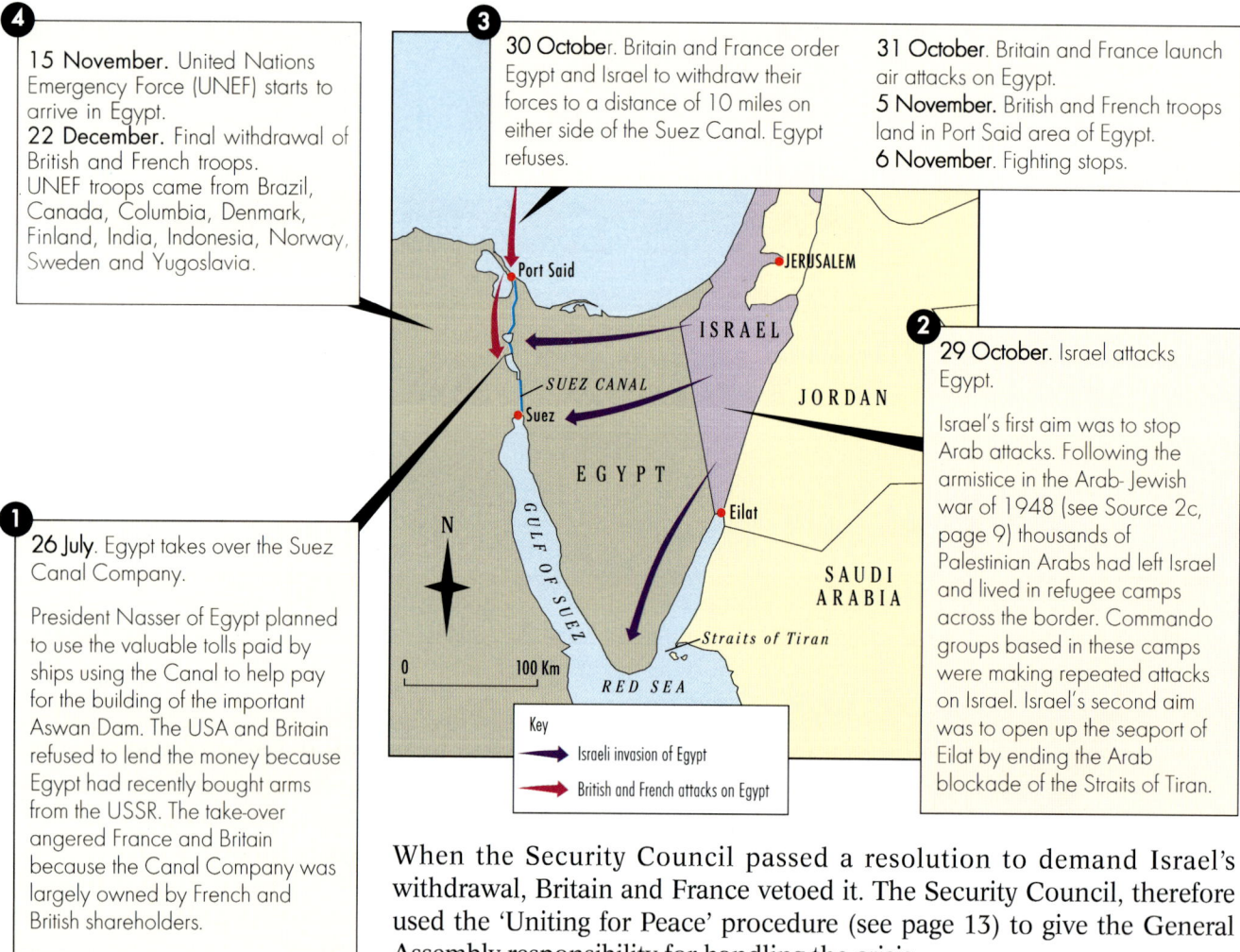

4

15 November. United Nations Emergency Force (UNEF) starts to arrive in Egypt.
22 December. Final withdrawal of British and French troops.
UNEF troops came from Brazil, Canada, Columbia, Denmark, Finland, India, Indonesia, Norway, Sweden and Yugoslavia.

3

30 October. Britain and France order Egypt and Israel to withdraw their forces to a distance of 10 miles on either side of the Suez Canal. Egypt refuses.

31 October. Britain and France launch air attacks on Egypt.
5 November. British and French troops land in Port Said area of Egypt.
6 November. Fighting stops.

2

29 October. Israel attacks Egypt.

Israel's first aim was to stop Arab attacks. Following the armistice in the Arab-Jewish war of 1948 (see Source 2c, page 9) thousands of Palestinian Arabs had left Israel and lived in refugee camps across the border. Commando groups based in these camps were making repeated attacks on Israel. Israel's second aim was to open up the seaport of Eilat by ending the Arab blockade of the Straits of Tiran.

1

26 July. Egypt takes over the Suez Canal Company.

President Nasser of Egypt planned to use the valuable tolls paid by ships using the Canal to help pay for the building of the important Aswan Dam. The USA and Britain refused to lend the money because Egypt had recently bought arms from the USSR. The take-over angered France and Britain because the Canal Company was largely owned by French and British shareholders.

Map labels: Port Said, JERUSALEM, ISRAEL, SUEZ CANAL, Suez, JORDAN, EGYPT, Eilat, GULF OF SUEZ, SAUDI ARABIA, Straits of Tiran, RED SEA, N, 0   100 Km

Key
→ Israeli invasion of Egypt
→ British and French attacks on Egypt

When the Security Council passed a resolution to demand Israel's withdrawal, Britain and France vetoed it. The Security Council, therefore used the 'Uniting for Peace' procedure (see page 13) to give the General Assembly responsibility for handling the crisis.

The General Assembly met in emergency session. The non-aligned nations were all hostile to the action taken by Britain and France. The Assembly called for a cease-fire and the withdrawal of troops. Lester Pearson, Canada's Foreign Minister, then proposed a new idea: a UN peacekeeping force to be provided entirely by smaller countries. On 4 November it was agreed to set up a United Nations Emergency Force (UNEF) on these lines. UNEF was given three tasks: first, to supervise the cease-fire; second, to arrange the withdrawal of forces; third, to make sure that Israel and Egypt kept to the agreements made in the 1948 armistice.

The Assembly asked the Secretary-General, Dag Hammarskjöld, to take responsibility for planning and running the operation. The Assembly also agreed some principles, suggested by Hammarskjöld, to guide the conduct and organisation of the operation. These were that:

- The UNEF was to act as a buffer between the two sides, not to fight either of them. Its soldiers would use their weapons only in self-defence.
- The commander of UNEF should be responsible directly to the General Assembly and/or the Security Council.
- UNEF troops should come only from states which were not permanent members of the Security Council.

Meanwhile, on 5 November, British and French troops parachuted into the Suez Canal zone. The fighting was stopped, not by the UN, which was powerless, but by the USA, which disapproved of the British and French action. When the British needed to borrow money urgently from the Americans on 6 November, they refused to lend it until the fighting was called off.

Ten days later UNEF troops started to arrive in Egypt. UNEF remained patrolling the cease-fire line until 1967 when the Egyptians asked it to leave.

Hungary

While the world's attention was focused on Suez, Soviet troops invaded Hungary to put down a revolt against Soviet control of the country. Members of the Security Council wanted to call for a withdrawal of Soviet troops and the General Assembly set up a Committee of Investigation. The USSR used its veto to block the Security Council resolution and refused to co-operate with the Committee. It also refused to allow Dag Hammarskjöld to visit the Hungarian capital, Budapest.

Questions

1 Ask your teacher for a copy of the chart 'The UN in Korea and Suez'. Complete it, following the instructions at the top of the sheet.

2 **a)** Look at your completed chart. What were the main differences between the UN's involvements in Korea and Suez?
   b) What do you think were the reasons for these differences?

3 Why was the UN able to intervene in Suez, but not in Hungary?

4 **a)** How did (i) the Suez Crisis, and (ii) the Hungarian Crisis show that a Security Council resolution alone was unlikely ever to stop a war?
   b) What does this suggest about the authority of the Security Council?

Unit 3 · The UN in the Congo

Source 1

UN soldiers firing on Katangan forces from the cover of their armoured car.

On 12 August 1960 the Secretary-General of the UN, Dag Hammerskjöld, took off in a white aircraft from an airport in the Congo Republic in central southern Africa. Four more planes carrying Swedish troops followed. The soldiers wore their national uniforms and the light blue helmets of a UN peacekeeping force.

A few hours later they reached their destination, Elisabethville, capital of the province of Katanga. As Hammarskjöld's plane circled the airfield, the voice of Moise Tshombe, President of Katanga, came onto the ground-to-air radio demanding that the UN troops turn back. On the ground the runway was ringed with machine guns and tanks manned by Belgian soldiers.

The UN Secretary-General ignored Tshombe's demands and his plane landed in the ring of guns. Hammarskjöld refused to leave the airport until he had seen his troops land safely. The 220 men disembarked and started to take over control of the airport from the Belgians. The next day a thousand more UN troops arrived in Katanga.

So began of one of the UN's most controversial operations, in which UN forces ended up fighting Katangan troops led by white mercenaries (Source 1). It was bound up in the UN's much wider involvement in a four-year crisis in the Congo Republic. This Unit is about that crisis, why the UN became involved in it, what impact the UN had and how its involvement has been portrayed by historians.

3.1 Background to the Congo Crisis

Patrice Lumumba. When the Belgians promised 'freedom in 30 years', Lumumba's speeches raised Congolese anger against their rule and were one cause of their sudden departure.

Source 3

Moise Tshombe. He got on well with Belgian officials and business people. Some of his enemies called him 'a European with a black skin'.

Sudden independence

The Congo was the part of Africa known today as Zaire. Until 1960 it was a Belgian colony. Although the Belgians had done much to develop health care and primary education, they had neglected higher education. There was not one Congolese doctor, engineer or senior government administrator; nor a single Congolese officer in the army. Despite this, early in 1960 the Belgians suddenly announced that the Congo was to become independent. They left only five months for the details to be arranged.

The new Republic of the Congo became independent on 30 June 1960. Patrice Lumumba (Source 2) became its Prime Minister, with Joseph Kasavubu as President.

Mutiny

Within a week of independence Congolese soldiers in the capital, Leopoldville, mutinied against their Belgian officers, complaining that self-rule had improved neither their pay nor their chance of becoming officers. The mutiny was followed by riots and attacks on Europeans.

This mutiny created the crisis that was to engulf the Congo for more than four years. Firstly, it weakened the new government because it lost its ability to maintain law and order. Secondly, it caused panic among the thousands of Belgians on whom the Congo still relied to run its civil, health and education services. As a result, the Belgian government sent paratroops to protect them. This was illegal, since the Congolese government had made no request for help.

A breakaway province

One Congolese leader, however, did ask for Belgian assistance. This was Moise Tshombe, President of the province of Katanga (Source 3). He did so without consulting Prime Minister Lumumba and almost immediately afterwards he declared Katanga an independent state. Katanga was the richest of the Congo's six provinces, providing about 45 per cent of the colony's total revenues under the Belgians. Most of this wealth came from Katanga's European-owned mines which produced 8 per cent of the world's copper and 60 per cent of its cobalt. Backed by the mine-owners, Tshombe intended to keep future revenues for Katanga.

Questions

1. What do you think a) Lumumba, and b) Tshombe thought about the Belgian government's decision to send troops back to the Congo when the Congolese Army mutinied? Explain your answers.

2. Most people in Belgium itself strongly supported the action. One reason was that they were angered by the news that some Congolese soldiers had attacked Belgians who lived and worked in the Congo. What other reasons do you think they might have had?

3. Why might the European mine-owners in Katanga have supported the government of Moise Tshombe?

3.2   The UN's response to the crisis

Lumumba and Kasavubu appealed to the UN. They had lost control of their army and needed help to restore order and keep essential services running. They wanted the Belgian troops to leave and they wanted to prevent the breakaway of their wealthiest province.

Members of the Security Council had different points of view on the Congo. The USA wanted to prevent Soviet interference there, but did not want to be seen to act directly on its own. But as it also wanted a government in the Congo friendly to the West, it strongly backed action by the UN.

The USSR saw the Congo Crisis as a chance to gain support among the non-aligned states by championing their cause. It supported UN intervention in order to be seen to be hostile to colonialism. It also wanted Lumumba's government to become a Soviet ally; but it did not want this to be obvious. It hoped to work on it under the cover of the UN's intervention.

The Afro-Asian states, represented on the Security Council by Tunisia, wanted to see the successful decolonisation of the Congo and to avoid any confrontation there between the great powers.

Britain and France both wanted stability in the Congo but were not sure about UN intervention. France opposed it from the start and argued that the USA, Britain and France should sort out the crisis between them. Britain broadly supported UN intervention but was always worried that this might open the way for UN involvement in its own African colonies. Britain was anxious, therefore, that UN action should not become interference in the Congo's internal affairs.

The Security Council acts

Dag Hammarskjöld called an urgent Security Council meeting about the Congo on 13 July 1960. He asked it to give aid and to consider the problem of law and order. During the seven-hour meeting, Hammarskjöld, helped by Mongi Slim of Tunisia, managed to push through a resolution authorising the creation of a UN force. The Security Council then asked the Secretary-General to organise the operation.

Already, before the meeting, he had asked Morocco, Tunisia, Ghana and Ethiopia to provide troops. When the meeting ended at 3.30 a.m. Hammarskjöld and his staff started work:

Source 4

Brian Urquhart, *A Life in Peace and War*, 1987.

Hammarskjöld, as usual, was the mainspring, telephoning all over the world for troops, aircraft, staging areas and supplies . . . setting up a command and staff organisation . . . . Three hours later, when we dispersed for breakfast, the operation was already under way.

■   What evidence is there in Source 4 and the information in the text that Hammarskjöld took the initiative in dealing with the Congo Crisis?

ONUC

The UN force, known by its French name, *Force de l'Opération des Nations Unies au Congo* (ONUC), at first consisted of about 4,500 soldiers from the African states of Ghana, Ethiopia, Guinea, Morocco and Tunisia. They were flown into the Congo by American, British and

Source 5

Swedish troops disembarking from a US Air Force 'Globemaster' at Elisabethville. The US Air Force airlifted 74,396 UN troops and 10,281 tonnes of cargo to or from the Congo.

1 Look at Source 5 and the information in the text about ONUC. Make a list of the similarities between the Congo peacekeeping operation and the one for Suez (pages 16–19).

2 Why do you think the two strict instructions given to ONUC forces made it especially difficult for them to carry out their tasks?

3 Why do you think: a) the USSR supported the idea that UN troops should attack Katanga; b) Dag Hammarskjöld refused to let them do so?

4 Why might the new African nations have decided to oppose Khrushchev's proposals about the job of Secretary-General?

Soviet aircraft. Later, units were added from other countries, notably India, Pakistan, Sweden and Ireland (Source 5).

ONUC troops were given three main tasks: to restore and maintain law and order; to prevent civil war; and to stop other countries from becoming involved in the Congo's affairs.

They were also given two very strict instructions:

- They were to use force only in self-defence.
- They were not to interfere in the Congo's internal affairs. In particular, this meant they could take no action which might support one group of Congolese against another.

The Katanga problem

At the request of the Security Council, the Belgians withdrew all their troops except those in Katanga. They argued that in Katanga they were helping to keep things peaceful. Lumumba then demanded that the UN should attack Katanga and force it to reunite with the rest of the country. Hammarskjöld refused, saying that the UN could not take sides in an internal dispute. Instead, as you have read, he personally led an operation to enable UN troops to enter Katanga peacefully.

Lumumba was furious and immediately asked the Soviet Union for transport planes to help him carry out his own attack. The Soviets agreed, but the attack failed. Shortly afterwards President Kasavubu dismissed Lumumba. Colonel Mobutu, the commander of Congolese troops in Leopoldville, then seized power in a military take-over. With Kasavubu's backing he ruled until February 1961.

The USSR and the new African nations

One of Dag Hammarskjöld's main aims during the Congo Crisis was to prevent the superpowers from intervening directly. So he was particularly worried by the USSR's direct military support for Lumumba. He feared, correctly, that the Soviets wanted to set up a new Congo government which they could control.

Meanwhile the Soviets said that the Belgians still in Katanga were trying to keep it under the influence of the West. They accused Hammarskjöld of being in the pocket of the West because he refused to involve UN troops in an attack on Katanga.

At the UN General Assembly in September 1960, when seventeen new African states were admitted to the UN, the Soviet leader, Nikita Khrushchev, launched a personal attack on Hammarskjöld, calling him a 'servant of the colonialists' and demanding the abolition of the post of Secretary-General.

In its place Khrushchev proposed a body consisting of three persons who would represent the West, the East and the non-aligned bloc. This would have given the Soviets a way of countering what they saw as the dominance of the West over the UN. Khrushchev miscalculated in hoping that the new African states would approve of this proposal. They did not. Instead, they repeatedly voted in support of Hammarskjöld and of his approach to the Congo Crisis.

The threat of civil war

At the beginning of 1961 the Congo was split between three rival groups, each claiming to be the government (Source 6). The central government in Leopoldville was in the hands of Colonel Mobutu, backed by President Kasavubu. Moise Tshombe continued to rule the breakaway province of Katanga. Meanwhile, in Stanleyville, Patrice Lumumba's supporters had set up a rival to the central government. Lumumba himself was arrested trying to reach Stanleyville and in January 1961 he was murdered while in the hands of Tshombe's supporters in Katanga.

Source 6

Rival groups and their backers in the Congo, 1961.

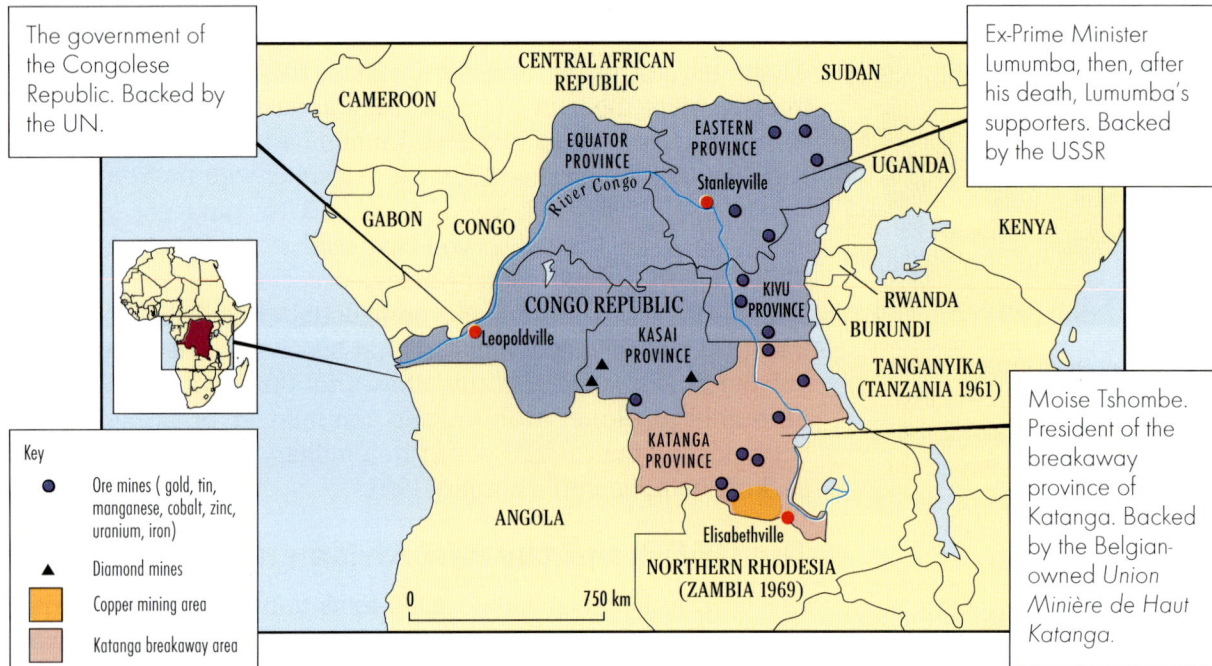

The government of the Congolese Republic. Backed by the UN.

Ex-Prime Minister Lumumba, then, after his death, Lumumba's supporters. Backed by the USSR

Moise Tshombe. President of the breakaway province of Katanga. Backed by the Belgian-owned *Union Minière de Haut Katanga.*

Key
- Ore mines (gold, tin, manganese, cobalt, zinc, uranium, iron)
- Diamond mines
- Copper mining area
- Katanga breakaway area

The Congo seemed about to break into three warring units, two backed by foreign powers. Tshombe had the approval of the Belgians, while the Soviets were ready to support the Stanleyville government. In February 1961, therefore, the Security Council ordered all foreign soldiers and advisers not under UN control to leave the Congo, and agreed to allow ONUC troops to use force to prevent a civil war. But it still did not authorise them to use force to reunite Katanga with the rest of the Congo.

In August the threat of civil war receded when two of the rival groups came together and the Congolese parliament, under ONUC protection, elected a new government led by Cyrille Adoula. Katanga, however, remained defiant.

Bloodshed in Katanga

The money from the mining companies in Katanga enabled Tshombe to pay white mercenary soldiers, especially Belgians, to train and lead his army. One of Adoula's first actions as the Congo's new Prime Minister was to order these mercenaries to leave Katanga. He believed they were encouraging Tshombe to defy the central government. He also asked the UN to help him to get rid of them.

In 'Operation Rumpunch', on 28 August, ONUC troops in Katanga started to round up the 500 mercenaries on their 'wanted' list. The Belgian Consul objected. He offered to ensure that the people on the list left the country voluntarily if the UN stopped the round-up. The UN agreed; but the Belgian Consul failed to carry out his side of the bargain.

On 13 September the UN tried again. This time they met armed resistance and fought a battle against mercenaries and the Katangan troops whom they led. The operation failed. Many people were shocked that a peacekeeping force had caused bloodshed. How could peacekeepers possibly justify the use of force? Lord Home, the British Foreign Secretary, complained that a stage had been reached:

Source 7

Lord Home, from a speech at Berwick, December 1961.

. . . when a large part of the organisation which is dedicated to peace openly condones aggression; when an organisation which was founded to sustain law and order encourages policies which must endanger it.

In return, Hammarskjöld explained that the UN had a duty to get rid of the white mercenaries who were preventing Tshombe from negotiating with the properly elected national government:

Source 8

Observer, 24 September 1961.

With the formation of the Adoula Government, the UN's duty to evict the Katangan mercenaries – a duty imposed by the Security Council resolution of last February . . . became inescapable.

Source 9

Rescue workers scramble among the wreckage of the UN airliner which was carrying Dag Hammarskjöld to Rhodesia.

Tshombe then fled to Rhodesia. Four days later Hammarskjöld also flew to Rhodesia to reason with Tshombe over his defiance of Adoula. As his plane prepared to land, it crashed, killing everyone on board (Source 9).

U Thant of Burma took over as Secretary-General and in November the Security Council for the first time gave the UN clear authority to use force to remove foreign mercenaries and political advisers from Katanga. In December 1961 ONUC forces went into action again. This time Tshombe agreed to negotiate with Adoula and U Thant ordered a cease-fire. A year later the talks were still going on and it took yet another UN attack in late 1962 to drive out the last of the mercenaries. Tshombe left the country and Katanga was reunited with the Congo Republic in January 1963.

The historian Peter Calvocoressi has recently portrayed the bloodshed in Katanga as an inevitable consequence of peacekeeping duties:

Source 10

Peter Calvocoressi, *World Politics Since 1945*, 1992.

In the Katanga operations the UN . . . suffered from the criticism that UN forces had come to secure order but had shed blood in the name of peace . . . [but] all police operations must envisage the use of force as an ultimate sanction [method of enforcing the law].

Questions

1 Use Sources 8, 10 and the information in the text.
a) Make a list of the arguments in favour of the UN's actions in Katanga.
b) Should peacekeepers should use force other than in self-defence? Why?

2 Look at the three aims given to ONUC forces (page 21). How successful do you think they had been by 1964 in carrying out each one?

3.3 Was the UN operation a success?

The UN's actions in the Congo stirred up controversy at the time and this is still reflected in the way British historians write about them today. This section is about some conflicting interpretations of the events. It is for you to judge their strengths and weaknesses and to think about how the differences have arisen.

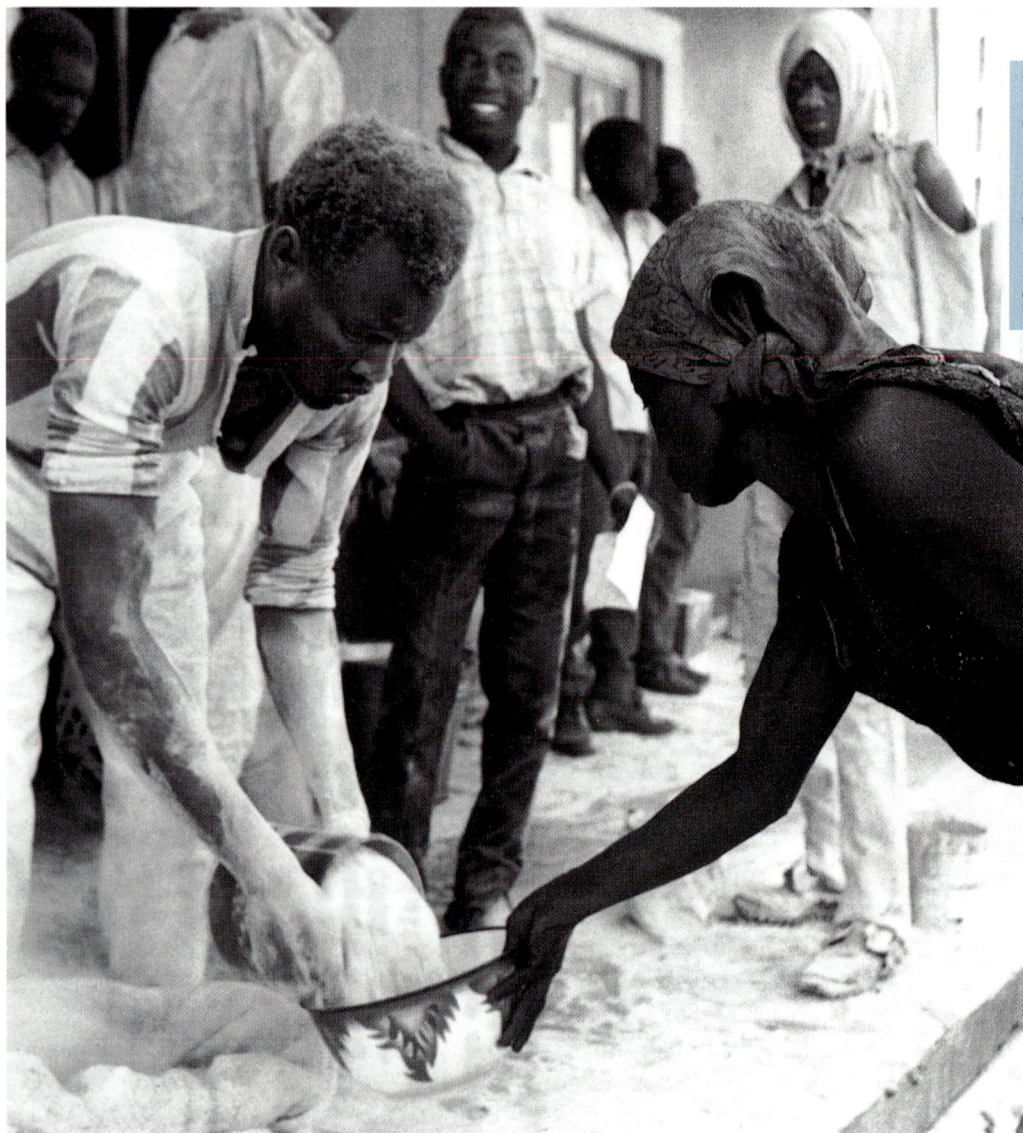

Source 11

The UN helped the government to run the Congo during the crisis. Its relief and medical workers helped to prevent famine and epidemics.

Different interpretations

Most British historians agree that the UN's work in the Congo outside the sphere of peacekeeping was very successful (Source 11); but they disagree about the peacekeeping operation itself. Some see the UN's actions as unsuccessful, claiming that it interfered unnecessarily in the Congo Republic's internal affairs, caused bloodshed and delayed the setting up of an effective government:.

Source 12

Paul Johnson, *Modern Times*, 1983.

If Hammarskjöld had done nothing and allowed Belgium to restore order, the crisis might have been quickly resolved with the minimum of bloodshed . . .. Instead the Secretary-General immediately set about creating and deploying a UN army, taken not from the Security Council powers (as the UN Charter clearly intended) but from the 'non-aligned' states from which Hammarskjöld drew his following.

Others see the UN operation as a considerable success:

Source 13

Peter Calvocoressi, *World Politics Since 1945*, 1992.

It achieved almost immediately its first aim of displacing [except from Katanga] the Belgians . . .. Its intervention also prevented intervention by individual states on their own account and enforced in one case, the Russian, a retreat; fears that Africa would become a new theatre for the Cold War were allayed [put aside] . . .. It could take credit for staving off civil wars in the Congo which would almost certainly have been worse but for the UN presence . . .. Finally, when the UN forces departed in June 1964 Katanga had not seceded [broken away].

The role of the Secretary-General

Behind Paul Johnson's and Peter Calvocoressi's portrayals of the ONUC operation lie their two very different views of Dag Hammarskjöld. Calvocoressi describes Hammarskjöld's death as an 'appalling calamity' because he was:

Source 14

Peter Calvocoressi, *World Politics Since 1945*, 1992.

. . . one of the half-dozen outstanding personalities in postwar international affairs.

By contrast, Johnson takes a wholly critical view of his actions:

Source 15

Paul Johnson, *Modern Times*, 1983.

It was Hammarskjöld's manifest [obvious] intention to cut the umbilical cord which linked the UN to the old wartime Western alliance, and to align the organisation with what he regarded as the new emergent force of righteousness in the world: the 'uncommitted nations'.

He argues that Hammarskjöld's role was crucial. When the Belgians sent their troops to restore order in the Congo:

Source 16

Paul Johnson, *Modern Times*, 1983.

Hammarskjöld saw his chance, turned angrily and decisively on the Belgians, and on 13 July, in front of the Security Council, denounced their troops as a threat to peace and order. The Secretary-General had been looking for an opportunity to expand the UN's role, and to ride to world government on a swelling tide of Third World emotion.

How accurate is this portrayal of Hammarskjöld's views? There is no doubt Hammarskjöld held strong opinions about the role of the UN. As a result of the Suez Crisis, for example, he believed that the smaller and non-aligned nations had an important role to play in UN affairs. He was also particularly concerned about the effects of the Cold War and wanted to keep the superpowers out of Africa (Source 17).

Source 17

From an unpublished letter, 1960. Quoted in Brian Urquhart, *Hammarskjöld*, 1973.

I have a feeling that Africa is a part of the world which at present is outside . . . the cold war . . . and I would like to see that part of the world remain outside.

Hammarskjöld argued that the UN should intervene whenever conflict arose in a part of the world where neither superpower was in control, but where they might try to compete for power.

He also believed that colonies should be given their independence as soon as possible and that the UN should be the protector of new nations. In a speech to the General Assembly, he said:

Source 18

Speech to General Assembly, 3 October 1961.

It is not the Soviet Union or, indeed, any other big powers who need the United Nations for their protection; it is all the others. In this sense the Organisation is first of all their organisation, and I deeply believe in the wisdom with which they will be able to use it and guide it.

Questions

1 Look at Sources 17 and 18.
a) What do they tell you about Hammarskjöld's views on: (i) the role of the UN in Africa; (ii) the relationship of the UN and the new nations?
b) How far do they, and the information in the text, support Johnson's claim in Source 16 that Hammarskjöld had been looking for an opportunity to: (i) 'expand the UN's role', (ii) 'ride to world government on a swelling tide of Third World emotion'?

2 Using the Sources and information on pages 19–24, explain: a) why a crisis occured in the Congo in 1960; b) why the UN become involved in it.

3 a) Use the Sources and information in this Unit to make lists of what you think were the UN's (i) successes and, (ii) failures in the Congo (your answer to Question 1 will also help you). Write a few sentences about each one.
b) Use your lists and notes to help you to write an essay in answer to this question, 'How successful was the UN's involvement in the Congo?'

4 What was the impact of: a) the superpowers; b) new nations; c) the Secretary-General on the UN's actions in the Congo between 1960 and 1964?

5 The UN's involvement in the Congo between 1960 and 1964 has been portrayed as: a) an efficient and successful response to a complicated international crisis; b) an unnecessary intervention, motivated by Dag Hammarskjöld's desire to expand the UN's role in world affairs, which caused needless bloodshed.
Choose one of these portrayals and say what you think are: (i) its strengths; (ii) its weaknesses. Give your reasons.

6 You are a historian who has been commissioned to write an account of how the UN became involved in the Congo and of its subsequent actions there. Explain what difficulties you will face in making sure that your account is an objective one.

Unit 4 · World conflicts, 1965–1985

By 1965 the UN was a very different organisation from the one its founders had imagined and it was obvious that it was not in a position to fulfill their hopes of preventing all wars between nations.

Nevertheless, the UN did attempt to stop wars and to limit their effects (Source 1). The organisation continued to use the limited peacekeeping means at its disposal: the passing of resolutions, the good offices of the Secretary-General, sanctions, observer missions, and peacekeeping forces. How successful was it?

Source 1

UN involvement in world conflicts, 1960–1985.

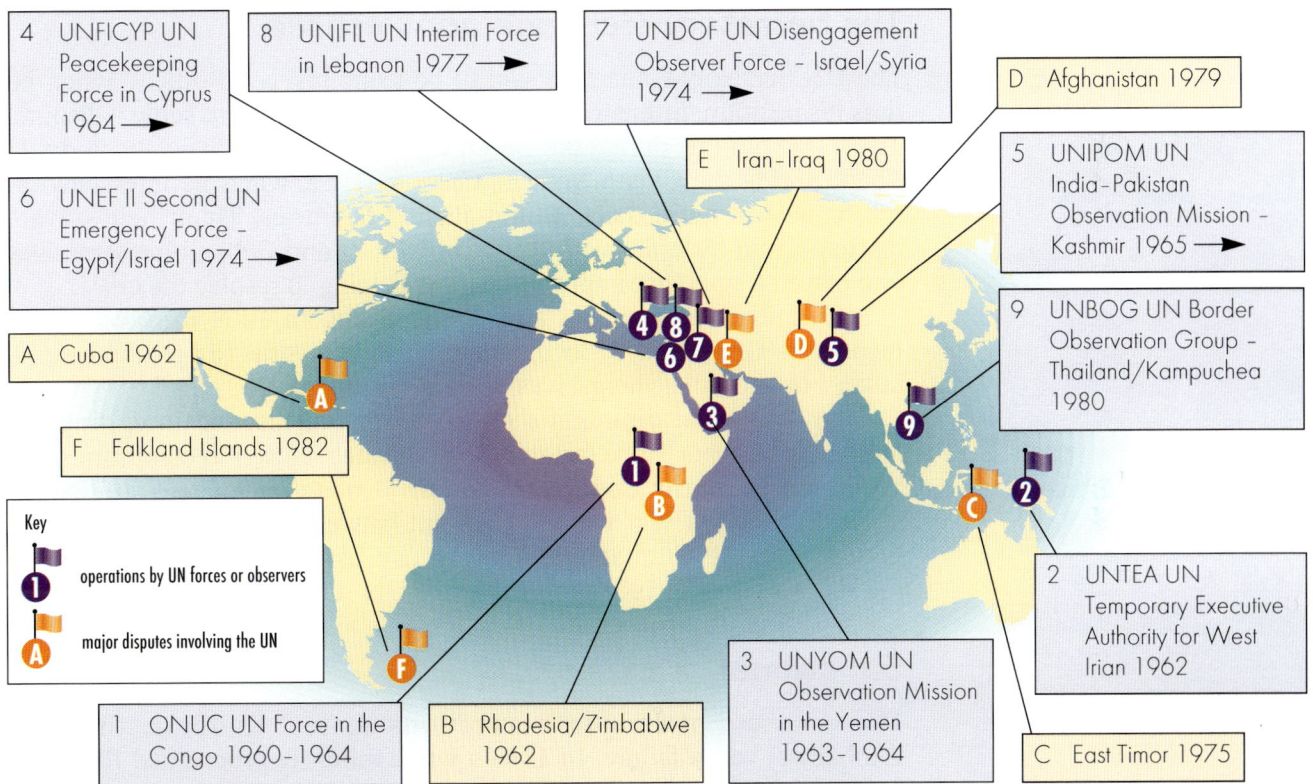

4 UNFICYP UN Peacekeeping Force in Cyprus 1964 →

8 UNIFIL UN Interim Force in Lebanon 1977 →

7 UNDOF UN Disengagement Observer Force - Israel/Syria 1974 →

D Afghanistan 1979

E Iran-Iraq 1980

5 UNIPOM UN India-Pakistan Observation Mission - Kashmir 1965 →

6 UNEF II Second UN Emergency Force - Egypt/Israel 1974 →

9 UNBOG UN Border Observation Group - Thailand/Kampuchea 1980

A Cuba 1962

F Falkland Islands 1982

Key

🚩1 operations by UN forces or observers

🚩A major disputes involving the UN

2 UNTEA UN Temporary Executive Authority for West Irian 1962

3 UNYOM UN Observation Mission in the Yemen 1963-1964

1 ONUC UN Force in the Congo 1960-1964

B Rhodesia/Zimbabwe 1962

C East Timor 1975

Successes and failures

Security Council resolutions

The Security Council continued to pass resolutions calling for cease-fires and troop withdrawals, but it still could not do much if the countries in dispute chose to ignore them. In 1979, for example, Soviet troops invaded and occupied Afghanistan in order to keep a pro-Soviet government in power there. The Security Council called for them to withdraw, but the USSR vetoed the resolution and kept troops in Afghanistan until 1988.

In 1982 Britain and Argentina fought a war over the disputed ownership of the Falkland Islands after Argentine forces had invaded and occupied them. Argentina ignored the Security Council's demand for the withdrawal of its forces. Britain then recaptured the islands by force, despite the Council's call for the dispute to be settled peacefully.

In the Middle East the UN was involved in two more Arab–Israeli wars, in 1967 and 1973, as well as in a long-running conflict in Lebanon. In each of the wars both sides obeyed cease-fire orders from the Security Council which set up further peacekeeping operations in 1974; but it was the USA rather than the UN which managed to bring together the Israelis and the Egyptians in successful peace talks in 1979.

Similarly, in 1966 the USSR helped to negotiate peace between India and Pakistan. War broke out between them in 1965 over the disputed territory of Kashmir. The Security Council ordered a cease-fire and troop withdrawals, and set up an observer mission to supervise both. The Council's orders were not fully obeyed until a meeting between the two heads of government in the USSR led to a truce agreement.

The Secretary-General's good offices

The UN Secretary-General is said to be using his 'good offices' when he uses his position, influence and diplomatic skills, to try to settle a dispute. Trygve Lie did this during the Berlin Crisis in 1948 (see page 8); so did U Thant during the Cuban Missiles Crisis in 1962, when he intervened at the request of more than 40 non-aligned countries. Thant held private discussions in his office with American, Soviet and Cuban representatives and played a small but important part in helping to resolve the crisis.

Such initiatives were not always successful. In 1969 Kurt Waldheim helped the Greek and Turkish communities in Cyprus to agree to resume talks; but the talks themselves were a failure. In 1982 Javier Pérez de Cuéllar's personal diplomatic efforts almost succeeded in ending the Falklands War, but at the last minute both sides refused to compromise.

Although Security Council resolutions demanding a cease-fire had no effect on the Gulf War which broke out between Iran and Iraq in 1980, Javier Pérez de Cuéllar managed to use his good offices to help to negotiate a peace in 1988. Thereafter the UN supervised the cease-fire.

Sanctions

The UN's use of economic sanctions against Rhodesia (modern Zimbabwe) was a failure. In 1965 a white minority proclaimed Rhodesia independent from Britain and set up a government which prevented the black majority from gaining their voting rights. The Security Council condemned the action and in 1966 imposed economic sanctions on Rhodesia in order to cut off essential supplies such as oil. The sanctions were ineffective, mainly because white South Africa refused to apply them. White rule ended in 1980 after the government had been defeated by black fighters in a seven-year guerilla war.

Observers and peacekeeping forces

UN observer missions were set up to keep watch on particular situations, usually once a cease-fire had been agreed, and to report on what they saw. They lacked the power to prevent fighting; but their presence often helped to keep the peace. For instance, the UN kept a Military Observer

Group in India and Pakistan (UNMOGIP) from 1948 following the outbreak of the dispute over Kashmir. The observers could not prevent fresh outbreaks of fighting in 1965 and 1971; but at other times their presence acted as a deterrent. They remain there today.

The UN continued to use peacekeeping forces to act as buffers between warring armies, with orders to fire only in self-defence. Although not at all what the founders of the UN had in mind, this aspect of its work was possibly its most successful, as well as its most difficult. The experience of the UN Peacekeeping Force in Cyprus (UNFICYP) showed both the strengths and the weaknesses of this approach to peacekeeping. The force was set up in 1964 to keep apart the Turkish and Greek communities, following a civil war which broke out between them when the British gave the island its independence in 1960. Its job was to prevent fighting and to maintain law and order. Not an easy task, according to this report from the Secretary-General:

Source 2

From the Report of the Secretary-General, 8 December 1966.

Since 7th June 1966, the United Nations civilian police have investigated more than 200 cases related to inter-communal strife. These include . . . cases of homicide [murder] and attempted homicide . . . alleged shooting at persons working in fields or from vehicles travelling through villages . . . assault . . . larceny [theft] and damage to property . . . bomb explosions and . . . investigations into the origins of forest fires.

Until 1974 UNFICYP managed to prevent major conflict, But when the Greek Cypriots tried to unite Cyprus with Greece and Turkish forces invaded the north of the island in support of the Turkish Cypriots, there was nothing it could do except to observe and to report events. The UN managed to arrange a cease-fire, but Cyprus was divided, with the northern third remaining under Turkish control (Source 3).

Reinforced to 6,000 troops, UNFICYP then stationed itself along the new dividing line. The cease-fire has held ever since. The UN force is still there today and numbers about 2,500 soldiers.

Source 3

A UN soldier in Cyprus escorting an elderly Greek woman across a bridge from the Turkish sector to the Greek sector.

Questions

1 Use the Sources and information in Unit 4 (pages 27–29). Make a list of what you think are i) the strengths, ii) the weaknesses of: a) Security Council resolutions; b) the Secretary-General's good offices; c) sanctions; d) observers and peacekeeping forces, as methods of UN peacekeeping between 1965 and 1985.

2 Use the information in Units 2, 3 and 4. What was the impact on the UN's peacekeeping role between 1945 and 1985 of: a) superpower rivalry; b) the UN's increasing membership?

3 How successful do you think the UN was in its peacekeeping role between 1945 and 1985?

4 How and why did the UN's peacekeeping role develop between 1945 and 1985?

Unit 5 · Creating a better world

5.1   The agencies of the UN

The founders of the UN intended it to create a better world in two main ways. Firstly, it was to keep the peace. Secondly, it was to help people everywhere to become more prosperous and better educated, and to live healthier and freer lives. In the words of the Charter:

Source 1

From Article 55 of the United Nations Charter, 1945.

The United Nations shall promote:

a) higher standards of living, full employment, and conditions of economic and social progress and development;
b) solutions of international economic, social, health and related problems and international cultural and educational co-operation; and
c) universal respect for, and observance of, human rights and fundamental freedoms for all without distinction as to race, sex, language or religion.

A network of special bodies working in many different fields has been set up to carry out this work (Source 3). Some are UN bodies which are directly controlled by the Economic and Social Council (ESC). Others, known as the Specialised Agencies of the UN, are independent organisations which are linked to the UN and have their work co-ordinated by the ESC. Some of these were founded as far back as the last century.

The rest of this Unit is about the work of the UN's agencies in attempting to deal with some of the major social and economic issues facing the world between 1945 and 1985. Some were successful in bringing about international co-operation on global issues. Others failed because some countries became very critical of their methods and refused to co-operate with them.

Source 2

Villagers taking fresh water from a hand-pump installed with the help of UNICEF.

Source 3

The major agencies, commissions and programmes of the UN system.

Major agencies, commissions and programmes of the UN system

Most of these have been created by decisions of the General Assembly, the Economic and Social Council, or both together.

International Communications

ICAO
International Civil Aviation Organisation 1947

IMO
International Maritime Organisation 1982 (1958)

ITU
International Telecommunications Union 1947 (1865)

UPU
Universal Postal Union 1947 (1875)

WMO
World Meteorological Organisation 1950 (1878)

Trade, Industry and Finance

GATT
General Agreement on Tariffs and Trade 1948

IBRD
International Bank for Reconstruction and Development. Also known as the World Bank 1944

IMF
International Monetary Fund 1944

UNCTAD
Conference on Trade and Development 1964

UNDIDO
Industrial Development Organisation 1965

Regional Economic Commissions

One each for: Africa; Asia and the Pacific; Europe; Latin America; and Western Asia

Functional Commissions

One each on: social development; human rights; drugs; the status of women; population; and statistics

Refugees

UNHCR
High Commissioner for Refugees 1951

UNRW
Relief and Works Agency for Palestine Refugees 1949

Atomic Energy

IAEA
The International Atomic Energy Agency 1957

Education and Training

UNESCO
Educational, Scientific and Cultural Organisation 1946

UNICEF
International Children's Emergency Fund 1946

ILO
International Labour Organisation 1946 (1919)

The Environment

IAEA
International Atomic Energy Agency 1957

UNEP
Environment Programme 1972

UNESCO
Educational, Scientific and Cultural Organisation 1946

UNICEF
International Children's Emergency Fund 1946

Labour and Working Conditions

ILO
International Labour Organisation 1946 (1919)

Health and Nutrition

IAEA
International Atomic Energy Agency 1957

WHO
World Health Organisation 1948

UNESCO
Educational, Scientific and Cultural Organisation 1946

UNICEF
International Children's Emergency Fund 1946

ILO
International Labour Organisation 1946 (1919)

FAO
Food and Agriculture Organisation 1946 (1943)

5.2   Social issues

Italian orphans eating a meal provided by UNICEF. Thousands of children all over Europe lost their parents as a result of the Second World War.

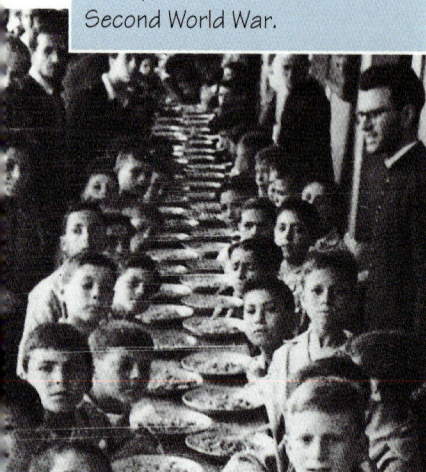

Refugees

Immediately after the Second World War the UN's agencies concentrated on helping to rebuild the lives of people living in war-torn Europe. When that was done they became more involved in assisting poor and developing countries. That remains their major task today.

The UN's work with refugees has followed this pattern. During the war millions of people were made homeless. The United Nations Relief and Rehabilitation Administration (UNRRA) was set up in 1943 to help to feed them and to find them new homes. Many refugees were gathered together in camps where food, shelter, medical care and education could be provided until they could find new homes and work.

Meanwhile, the United Nations International Children's Emergency Fund (UNICEF) was set up in 1946 especially to help children affected by the war (Source 4). In 1953 UNICEF became a permanent organisation.

unicef

Purpose
To help children and young people worldwide, particularly in devastated and developing countries, with educational and health care. Especially 'to help children who are in the greatest need – the poorest of the poor'.

Structure
An agency responsible to the UN. All staff are members of the UN Secretariat. All its money comes from gifts and from fund-raising efforts, none from the UN budget.

Some major UNICEF projects
- Health education, especially for women and girls because of their central role in family life. Training village health workers to give instruction about matters such as water purification, sanitation and balanced diet.
- Setting up maternity and child health centres in over 100 countries.
- The International Year of the Child (1979). A campaign to raise awareness about the scale of the problems worldwide.

Source 5

The United Nations International Children's Emergency Fund (UNICEF).

The refugee problem in Europe was solved by the early 1950s, but by that time a new one had arisen in the Middle East. In 1948 the war between Arabs and Jews caused 800,000 Arabs to leave Palestine (see Source 2c, page 9). The UN immediately set up its Relief and Works Agency (UNRWA) to deal with the problem, which later became worse as a result of further Arab–Israeli wars.

By the 1960s the emergence of new nations in Africa was creating a massive refugee problem there too. In 1966 the UN High Commissioner for Refugees (UNHCR) estimated that the UN was dealing with more than 600,000 refugees in Africa and more than one million in the Middle East and Asia.

Health

Source 6

The World Health Organisation (WHO).

Purpose
To co-ordinate the fight against disease and medical research. To set drug and vaccine standards. To provide its members with technical help, advice and information. Main aim, 'the attainment by all peoples of the highest possible level of health'.

Structure
Run by a Director-General from its headquarters in Geneva. Has six regional offices worldwide. Its governing body is the World Health Assembly, which meets every May. There were 158 member countries in 1985 (that is, all UN members except the USSR).

Some major projects
- Attacks on major diseases such as malaria (from 1955), smallpox (from 1959), tuberculosis (from 1960).
- Helping governments to set up health services in developing countries. Training doctors, nurses, technicians and health administrators to work in them.
- Programmes to immunise all the world's children against six 'child-killers' – measles, diphtheria, whooping cough, tetanus, polio and TB. Approximately one million lives saved each year.

The World Health Organisation (WHO) has led the efforts of UN agencies to bring about international co-operation to attack diseases and to improve the standard of people's health worldwide (Sources 2 and 6). In 1985 the UN reported that:

Source 7

Within Our Reach, Highlights of the Economic and Social Work of the United Nations 1945–1985.

Since 1950, life expectancy has advanced by almost 20 years and child mortality has fallen by two thirds.

One of WHO's first priorities was to try to eliminate the massive epidemics of diseases such as cholera, malaria and smallpox which regularly claimed the lives of millions of people, especially in the poorer countries. The most successful campaign was against smallpox, which used to kill about two million people a year. As a result of a vaccination programme started in 1959 smallpox was eradicated by 1980. In the words of the UN, this was:

Source 8

Within Our Reach, Highlights of the Economic and Social Work of the United Nations 1945–1985.

Preventive medicine The practice of medicine with the aim of keeping off disease.

. . . a victory for hundreds of thousands of health workers in many different countries. WHO staff alone were drawn from 73 different countries. It represents a triumph of international co-operation and preventive medicine.

Source 9

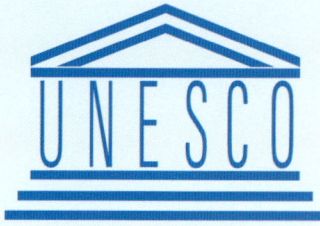

Purpose
To contribute to peace in the world by using education, science and culture to promote co-operation among nations and to increase respect for justice, the rule of law and human rights.

Structure
Its headquarters are in Paris. A General Conference of members meets every two years to decide policy, programme and budget. There were 157 member countries in 1985 (that is, all UN members except the USA and the UK.

Some major projects
- Literacy programmes (to teach people to read and write).
- Improving education by training teachers and equipping schools.
- Searching for ways of improving water supplies in poorer, developing countries (the International Hydrological Project).
- Research into the currents and make-up of the Indian and Atlantic Oceans (International Oceanographic Commission).
- The rescue of the Nile temples.

The United Nations Education, Scientific and Cultural Organisation (UNESCO).

Education and literacy

The job of the United Nations Education, Scientific and Cultural Organisation (UNESCO) is to use education, science and culture to contribute to peace and co-operation among nations (Source 9). UNESCO aims to break down ignorance and prejudice, for, as the opening statement of its constitution (set of rules) puts it:

Source 10

From the Constitution of UNESCO, 1946.

Since wars begin in the minds of men, it is in the minds of men that the defences of peace must be constructed.

One of UNESCO's major campaigns has been, and still is, to teach people to read and write. It set up its first literacy programmes in colonies which were on their way to independence. Its focus has remained on the poorer and less developed countries (Source 11). It also works with UNICEF to promote primary education for everyone in all countries.

Source 11

A literacy class in Ethiopia. In 1970 more than 90 per cent of Ethiopians were illiterate. By 1985, thanks to volunteer literacy workers, 70 per cent of Ethiopians could read and write.

■   This picture comes from a UN publication for schools called *Teaching about Literacy*.
a) What do you think it is intended to show?
b) How reliable do you think it is as historical evidence?

Questions

1 Using the Sources and information on pages 30–34, find two examples of ways in which UN agencies have contributed to international co-operation and write a paragraph to describe each one.

2 Using Sources 4, 6 and 9 and the information in the text:
a) Find examples of different UN agencies working in the same field.
b) What do you think might be (i) the advantages and (ii) the disadvantages of this?

5.3 Economic issues

Post-war reconstruction

Immediately after the Second World War the nations of the West, which dominated the UN, concentrated on rebuilding the economic life of those countries most affected by the war. Consequently, the UN's agencies concentrated on this too (Source 12).

The International Bank for Reconstruction and Development (IBRD) and the International Monetary Fund (IMF), which had both been founded in 1944 to help countries to develop their industry and trade after the war, started their operations. In addition, a number of countries signed an agreement called the General Agreement on Tariffs and Trade (GATT). This aimed to help countries to increase the amount of trade between them by laying down the rules of world trade.

The needs of developing countries

By 1960 the UN agencies had more or less completed their task of post-war reconstruction. At the same time, as the European empires broke up, many new nations were emerging with their own economic needs. The UN agencies, therefore, took on the task of providing them with the administrative and technical help which they needed.

The governments of these developing nations wanted their political freedom to be matched by rapid economic growth. Both they and the Western experts whose job it was to help them agreed on the way forward. They assumed that the right thing to do was to develop the kind of industries and technologies which had made the countries of the West so rich.

In fact this approach produced many failures. Few countries were ready to industrialise. In any case, the use of the latest and most costly Western technology was very often the wrong way to solve an economic problem in a country with its own particular society and way of life. Twenty years later, UN agencies were taking a different approach:

Source 12

Modern spraying equipment to help control the Colorado potato beetle in Poland. UNRRA distributed modern machinery, given by members of the UN, to those most in need of it.

Source 13

Within Our Reach, Highlights of the Economic and Social Work of the United Nations 1945–1985.

Technology by itself is no longer seen as the automatic problem solver. More than ever before, emphasis is being placed on appropriate technology, with simple, rugged village hand pumps having as much collective impact as the hydroelectric dam at a fraction of the cost.

Source 14

The Food and Agriculture Organisation (FAO).

The UN also realised that the needs of farmers in rural areas were being neglected. This led to crises in agriculture and food production which the Food and Agriculture Organisation (FAO) attempted to tackle.

Purpose
To raise levels of nutrition, to improve food production and distribution and to improve the lives of people living in the countryside. To increase the effectiveness of agriculture, forestry and fisheries.

Structure
Run by a Director-General from its headquarters in Rome. It has nine regional offices and over 70 smaller ones. There were 158 member countries in 1985 (that is, all UN members except the USSR).

Some major projects
- Freedom From Hunger Campaign (1960s) to raise money for projects in developing countries.
- World Food Programme (began 1963). A long-term plan to tackle world food needs. Still in progress.
- Co-ordination (since 1960) of the attack on locusts in Africa and the Middle East.
- Research projects. For example, on soils, irrigation, fertilizers and new types of wheat, barley and rice.

■ Using Sources 13 and 14 and the information in the text, explain how and why the UN's approach helped the developing countries change.

The North–South divide

Between 1955 and 1965, 43 colonies of the European empires gained their independence and joined the UN as new nations. You have seen already that this changed both the UN's approach to peacekeeping and the work of the UN's agencies. It also made a big difference to the topics that were discussed at the UN. From about 1960 the debates were increasingly about matters which the new nations felt were important to them. These were not always matters which the older established nations, the founding members of the UN, thought were important or wished to discuss.

Source 15

The North–South divide. The North included most of the countries in the two rival camps of East and West as well as Japan, Australia and New Zealand. The countries in the South were often referred to as 'developing'. In fact some were, and still are, the poorest in the world and were hardly developing at all, while by the 1980s others, such as South Korea and Singapore, were known as the 'newly industrialised nations' and were richer than several in the North.

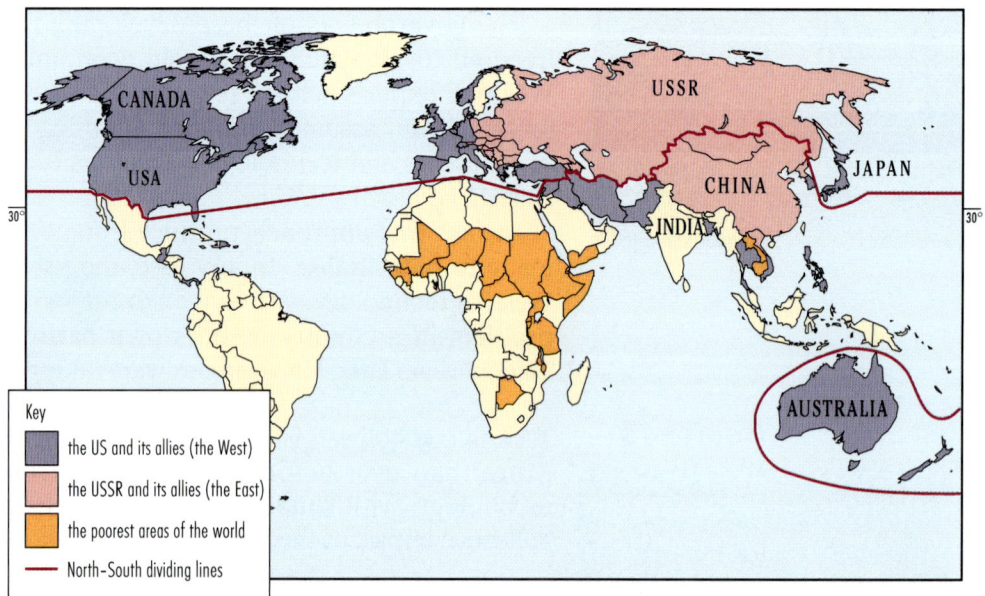

Key
- the US and its allies (the West)
- the USSR and its allies (the East)
- the poorest areas of the world
- North-South dividing lines

Possibly the topic which the new nations regarded as the most important concerned the relationship between the rich, developed, countries of the world and the poor, developing, ones. This issue came to be known as the North–South divide because the rich countries tend to be in the North and the poor ones in the South (Source 15).

The new nations argued that rich countries exploited poor countries by buying raw materials from them cheaply. Despite this, they said, the finished products from the rich countries were too expensive for poor countries to buy. They also argued that agencies such as the World Bank (IBRD), the IMF and the GATT did a good job for the trade and financial position of the countries of the North but did very little to help those of the South.

A 'New International Economic Order'?

1 In a discussion about the New International Economic Order what arguments might have been used: a) in its favour by a representative of the South; b) against it by a representative of the North?

2 Why did nothing come of the NIEO?

3 Why might the issues involved in the North–South divide be important for the North as well as for the South?

In 1964 the UN set up a new agency, the UN Conference on Trade and Development (UNCTAD), to promote trade between countries at different stages of development in order to speed up the economic growth of the developing countries. UNCTAD argued that the only way to do this was for the rich nations to agree to reorganise the world's economy so that the South would have a better share of trade, industry, bank loans, shipping, and so on. In 1974 the UN General Assembly accepted a declaration drawn up by UNCTAD demanding a 'New International Economic Order' (NIEO) along these lines.

The problem was that the rich nations of the North had very little respect for UNCTAD, which they saw as the mouthpiece of the new nations, rather than as an agency that had any interest in or respect for their own positions. Also, they knew that UNCTAD had no power to put its ideas into practice. It blamed the North for everything that was wrong and it announced what ought to happen instead, but it failed to set up serious negotiations between the countries of the North and the South. The developing countries had the voting power in the General Assembly to pass a declaration calling for the NIEO, but without the support of the North very little could change.

Continued divisions

Very little did change. Most Northern states thought that the NIEO was the wrong answer to the problem, quite apart from the fact that they put their own interests higher than those of the South. Then, in any case, a slump in the world economy in the 1980s caused them to try to protect their own economies at the expense of the South, for example by controlling the amount of goods they imported from Southern countries. They also insisted that developing countries to which they had lent massive sums of money in the 1970s should pay back their debts. In the 1980s, therefore, the countries of the South saw a complete collapse of their hopes for economic improvement through UN action. It was clear that, once again, the members of the United Nations were in fact divided.

Questions

How have: a) the emergence of new nations; b) the needs of developing countries; c) the responses of developed countries, influenced the social and economic work of the UN?

Unit 6 · Crisis in the UN

6.1   The 'politicisation' of the UN

By the 1980s there was further disagreement in the UN. The West claimed that through the actions of the developing countries the UN was becoming 'politicised', by which it meant that some of the agencies of the UN were becoming involved in political issues which were not their concern.

The Arab–Israeli conflict

Most African and Asian states, for example, had opposed the new state of Israel. When, in 1967, Israel occupied land belonging to Syria, Jordan and Egypt their hostility increased and in 1975 a UN General Assembly resolution denounced Israel's policy towards the Arabs as 'racist'.

After that, various agencies adopted anti-Israeli policies. WHO expressed concern at the poor health of Arabs living in the occupied territories and called on the Israelis to stop establishing settlements there. The International Labour Organisation (ILO) said that any occupation of territory was a violation of human and trade union rights and condemned Israel's actions. The USA then withdrew from membership of the ILO, saying that it had acted beyond the purposes for which it had been set up.

Source 1

The International Labour Organisation (ILO).

Purpose
To improve living and working conditions and promote employment worldwide. Also responsible for setting international standards for the protection of workers and the improvement of their conditions.

Structure
Its Conference of members includes representatives of employers and workers as well as of governments. There were 150 member countries in 1984. Member states must ask their parliaments to agree to ILO's new rules about international work standards. They must report back if they do not agree.

Some major projects
- Andes Indian Project (from 1954) to improve the living and working conditions of very poor Indian people in South America.
- Training refugees in Burundi, in central southern Africa, in agriculture and rural crafts so that they could earn their own living (1964).
- World Employment Programme (from 1969) to increase the number of useful jobs in the world and help to meet people's basic needs.
- Danger symbols. A series of warning signs that could be understood throughout the world even by people unable to read.

UNESCO

UNESCO's work also proved controversial. Some of its projects, such as the scheme to rescue the Nile temples in Sudan commanded general support in the UN. But Western nations objected when, in 1977, UNESCO attempted to set up a 'New World Information and Communications Order' (NWICO) which aimed to move control of services such as radio, television and newspaper networks away from the developed to the developing countries. Britain and the USA withdrew from membership of UNESCO in 1984 and 1985 because they believed it trespassed into political issues and wasted its money, 25 per cent of which was contributed by the USA in the first place.

Questions

1   What arguments might a critic have used to attack the actions of: ILO and WHO over the Arab–Israeli conflict; b) UNESCO over NWICO?

2   How might a supporter have defended them in each case?

6.2 Money and votes

Criticism of the UN's agencies was not all one way. The developing countries claimed that the USA was using its influence to block loans from the World Bank and the IMF to countries which it opposed, such as Cuba and Vietnam, because they had communist governments or were friendly with the USSR. This confirmed their view that these important financial agencies were really controlled by the Western nations.

The conflicts within the UN came to a head around the question of the amount of money each country contributed to the organisation. In 1985 the USA, as the world's wealthiest country, contributed 25 per cent of the UN's total budget.

Since the USA disagreed with the developing African and Asian countries over so many issues, and since those countries had a majority within the UN, the Americans decided to suggest a new voting system for the UN. Instead of one nation one vote, they proposed that each nation should have a number of votes according to the size of its contribution to the budget. Thus each member state would have influence within the UN according to how much it paid in.

The developing nations opposed this idea bitterly, since they wished to reduce the influence of the developed nations, not extend it. They also pointed out that there were several different ways of looking at budget contributions (see Source 2).

In 1985 the UN celebrated its fortieth anniversary; but the celebrations could not disguise the fact that the UN was in crisis. The following year the crisis deepened when the USA halved its contribution to the UN budget, partly because of the USA's own economic problems and partly because it objected to the influence of the developing countries on the policies of the UN and its agencies. In response, the UN had to dismiss 1,700 staff and cut back on most aspects of its work around the world.

Source 2

The top ten contributors to the UN's Regular Budget in 1984. From *United Nations: Image and Reality*, 1986.

SYSTEM A Worked out by total number of US dollars paid	SYSTEM B Worked out per head of the population	SYSTEM C Worked out as a percentage of the national income
USA	Norway	Gambia
Japan	Denmark	Equatorial Africa
West Germany	Sweden	Comoros
Italy	Qatar	Uganda
Canada	Netherlands	Guinea-Bissau
United Kingdom	Saudi Arabia	Norway
USSR	Finland	Grenada
France	Switzerland	Liberia
Sweden	Canada	Maldives
Netherlands	Libya	Samoa

Questions

1   Look at Source 2. As a method of working out the top ten contributors to the UN Regular Budget: System A favours the richest countries: System B favours wealthy countries with fairly small populations: System C favours poorer countries.

a) What are the arguments for and against each of the three systems?
b) (i) Why might the USA object to system C? (ii) Why might Gambia object to system A?
c) Which system do you think is the fairest?
d) What do you think are the arguments for and against allocating votes at the UN according to the size of a nation's contribution to the Regular Budget?

2   a) How might a representative of the USA have defended its decision to reduce its contribution to the UN in 1986?
b) How might a critic have responded?

6.3 United Nations?

Thus, in its forty-first year the UN was as divided within itself as it had ever been, and, as always, its divisions reflected those in the world it was supposed to be helping to unite. East confronted West and both were confronted by the South. As several historians have pointed out, the UN is the creation of its members and can act effectively only to the extent that its members demand and permit. The UN will always stand for the hope of a better world; equally, the world will always get the UN it deserves.

Questions

1   Use the Sources and information in Units 5 and 6. How successful do you think the UN's agencies have been in bringing about international co-operation to tackle world issues?

2   What do you think were the arguments, in 1985, for and against: a) the developing countries; b) the developed countries, continuing to support the work of the UN's agencies?